The Aggressive Adolescent
Clinical and Forensic Issues

The Aggressive Adolescent
Clinical and Forensic Issues

Daniel L. Davis, PhD

The Haworth Press
New York • London • Oxford

The Haworth Press, Inc., 10 Alice Street, Binghamton, NY 13904-1580

Cover design by ????

Library of Congress Cataloging-in-Publication Data

Davis, Daniel L.
    The aggressive adolescent : clinical and forensic issues
        p.   cm.
    Includes
    ISBN 0-

This work is respectfully dedicated to my wife, Heidi, my son Josh, to my family, and to all the youth and families that have taught me so much. I hope in some small way, this effort can be of benefit to those who read it and those whom they serve.

CONTENTS

Confidentiality Statement

The clinical examples and case histories presented in this manuscript are derived from actual case histories. However, all possible identifying information has been masked and modifications have been made to assure the anonymity of the youth portrayed. Although the resulting case histories accurately illustrate and reflect the type of case discussed, any similarity to an existing person, as a result of the changes made, is purely coincidental.

Clinical Prologue

THE YOUNG MAN IN A BODY CAST

When I last saw him, he was still in restraints, although he was on his way from the juvenile correctional facility. They always did that at this institution. The youth remained under the strict custody of the state until the last minute before freedom. Then, as was the way for all of those who left this place, he would be dressed in nondescript state issued clothing and his property would be put in a brown paper bag with his name and institutional number written on it.

The first time I saw him was in the medical facility of the institution. He was lying on a bed with his hands and feet were restrained with leather cuffs. He wore a fiberglass body shield about his abdomen. He had recently returned from a hospital as a result of treatment for one of a long series of self-inflicted wounds to his stomach area. This time, he nearly died. His small intestines had spilled out of his body. Much of them were removed due to the infection that resulted. If he did this to himself again, he would likely die.

Before I met him, I had reviewed his clinical chart as well as his institutional "jacket": the administrative file of his lengthy incarceration in the juvenile correctional system. From an identification picture taken five years previously, his youthful, defiant eyes seemed to look back. His hair was combed carefully and his chino shirt was buttoned all of the way to the top. Now, before me, lay a man-child whose skin color was the pale, washed pallor of too much time "inside," away from the sun. Officially, five years ago at age twelve he stole a car.

His journey, however, began long before. His biological father was unknown. His mother had married a violent alcoholic who physically and sexually abused him beginning at age two. Child Welfare system involvement began when, at age four, he was taken to the hospital as a result of a broken arm inflicted in a beating by his stepfather. Abuse was, in the terms of Children's Services, "substantiated" and a caseworker was assigned to the family. The beatings and sexual abuse continued unseen by a succession of overworked social workers until, as a result of his out of control behavior, he was placed in a foster home. There, he set fires, fought frequently with his peers, and often ran away from the foster home. The school system, because of his poor grades and attention span, evaluated him. He was found to have a learning disability, dyslexia, and was described as having attention-deficit disorder. His step-father deserted his mother and she, when he was seven, committed suicide. At the foster home, his nightmares caused him to scream nearly every night. After having been discovered sexually abusing the foster parent's dog, he was placed in a residential treatment center. However, two months later, the county tax levy for children's services was voted down and the agency began cost-cutting efforts. He was taken from the residential treatment center and placed in a much less expensive group home. From that point on, his out of control behavior would cause him to bounce between the detention home and a succession of group homes and foster care settings. When he stole the car at age twelve, the judge, seeing no other resources had him committed to the state juvenile correctional system.

Now, at seventeen, he lay bound head and foot, wrapped in fiberglass. We met at first on a daily basis. We talked of his life. I learned that there was life left in him. But, mostly, there was anger. In a way, it was the anger that kept him going, but paradoxically, threatened to be his death. I learned that, because of this anger, he had so terribly mutilated himself that his arms, legs, and neck were leathery with scars. But, he had never hurt another person. His anger was focused upon himself. He was filled with self-blame and felt completely out of control. In fact, as I later learned, his self-mutilation was not only a release of his rage, but it was the only pain that he could control. Physical pain that which he could feel in spite of his disassociation was far less discomforting than the psychological pain he endured each day. He had learned that the experience of self-mutilation both distracted him from his emotional pain and caused the staff of the large institution to have to respond to him.

Mostly, I listened to him. He tried to talk of his anger. Soon, we found that it was, for him, safer to draw out his thoughts and feelings. Sometimes, after an intense memory, he would tear up his drawing and throw it as far as he could. We would use his drawings to either talk about or draw other ways of managing his feelings. After a while, we did "family sessions" over the telephone with the one set of foster parents who had maintained contact with him. They made no promises about taking him back, but also did not reject the idea.

In time, he promised me that if I allowed his body cast to be removed, that he would try his best to not hurt himself. We drew up an anger plan. He returned from the hospital to the correctional institution. He kept his word. He moved up through the levels. He was granted a conditional release back to the foster parents who had, by that time, joined in actual family sessions with us. I remember when he left. As I often do, I asked him to write me and let me know how he was doing. I received one, maybe two letters. Since then, I have not heard from him. In this business, sometimes this is how you define success. . .

The treatment for severely emotionally and behaviorally disturbed youth and juvenile offenders is perhaps the most challenging and rewarding field in the mental health profession. I am always amazed when people ask me how can I work in such places? When you have the opportunity to serve where you are so needed . . . how can you not go to such places? Why is it that, in other health care fields, such as medicine, the best and the brightest work with the worst cases such as cancer or heart transplants? Yet, in mental health, we spend so little of our time with those who need us the most?

One does not enter into the process of treatment of these youth because they are attractive clients and because the places that keep them are comfortable places to work. One comes to such places precisely because they are not like that and we are about change. And, in coming to such places, if one listens, one learns that, beyond all else, we are more alike than different. With that, there is hope.

Acknowledgements

The author would like to gratefully acknowledge the support, teaching and inspiration drawn from many persons whom he has had the good fortune to know and hopefully from whom he has learned. I wish to thank first of all, Larry E. Cox, Professor of Psychology at Otterbein College without whom I never would have entered into this profession. As well, I wish to thank George Borelli, PhD, a master therapist and teacher and Harold Pepinsky, PhD, who guided me with care and insight through my graduate years. And, to Stanley L. Brodsky, PhD, who I greatly admire and aspire to his abilities as a teacher and therapist, I express my sincere gratitude.

To my parents, my aunt "Bebelle," thank you for all of your support and guidance throughout the years. Character has been built, I suppose. To my best friend, Lucinda, who has taught me so very much about therapy and myself. To my son, Josh, as he finds his way through the ebb and flow of higher education, thank you for who you are. Lastly, to my wife and center, Heidi: I love you more than I have words.

The Parable of Nasrudin

Nasrudin happened upon six foolish men who were standing next to an elephant. "Tell me, kind sirs," asked Nasrudin, "what is the nature of the beast which is beside you?" The first foolish man placed his hand upon the trunk of the elephant and described the elephant as long and cylindrical. The second man grabbed the tail and said, "No, an elephant is long and slender, like a rope." The third man held on to the ear and proclaimed the elephant to be wide and slender. Then the fourth man protested loudly while touching the leg and said, "No, an elephant is round and stout. Just then the fifth man who touched the body cried out even louder, "No an elephant is huge and broad." Lastly, sixth man, who was facing the other way laughed out loud and stated "You fools, I have searched and searched. There is no such thing as an elephant." And Nasrudin left them arguing loudly amongst themselves. . . (Ornstein, 1986)

This well-known Sufi parable is best known in the version that refers to six blind men. It is a story that I frequently used as an introduction in workshops on the treatment of violent persons. One time, after such a presentation, a very kind visually impaired person who had attended the talk sought me out. She told me, gently, how much the use of blind men in the story offended her. So, I modified the story to use six foolish men (figuring that foolish people would be unaware that they were being picked upon).

The point of the story is, of course, that a violent, troubled youth has many parts to him or to her. But, often, we only see the violent, resistive, angry actions of that person. This is, naturally, because such behaviors are immediate and intense in their effect upon us. These youth make us feel angry, frustrated, and inadequate. We lose hope: both in the ability of the youth to change and in our ability to effect any positive change.

1

When we see only the resistant and aggressive behaviors of the youth, we often then ignore the positive, resilient, and malleable qualities. When we do that, we cannot see that these youth can and will change and that we may be privileged to be part of that process. The only way, however, that we can meaningfully intervene in the lives of these youth is if we see our youth as whole, total persons. We cannot simply focus upon a single isolated characteristic such as violence. In short, that which confronts us in today's increasingly violent society demands that we see all of that which stands before us, not just a part of the elephant.

It is equally important to keep in mind that what motivates and drives these youth are often the very same things to which we all respond. We share common needs, desires, and aspirations. Frequently, for a therapist, these youth, when they do turn their lives around, become our most rewarding clients. For that to happen, we must always keep in mind the commonalties we share with these youth, rather than what seems to be an impossible gulf between us.

Introduction

Mental Health counselors in both public and private agencies today confront increasingly aggressive youth. These youth often pose significant legal risks for the counselor who provides mental health services. The youth are typically quite violent and often unpredictable in thinking and in behavior. They often have significant histories of neglect, physical, and sexual abuse and mental illness. Additionally, these youth are typically not responsive to traditional mental health or correctional intervention methods. The violent behavior of these youth also poses a number of significant risks to staff members and other youth or community residents. Because of the increasing "criminalization" of behavior that was once ascribed to mental illness, many seriously mentally ill youth are now involved in the juvenile or the adult criminal justice system. Accordingly, many mental health counselors now find themselves either working in a criminal justice setting or frequently dealing with criminal justice agencies. As the rates of persons sent to adult and juvenile justice facilities continues to increase, clinical mental health counselors will increasingly be required to be familiar with forensic mental health issues.

The problems of the violent mentally ill youth are not restricted, of course, to institutional settings. In past times, such youth were often seen as being untreatable in either community or residential settings. Now for many private, community based, treatment facilities it is no longer realistic or practical to exclude such youth from treatment settings. In today's treatment environment, the influence of managed care, of "no reject-no eject" philosophies and the sheer numbers of these youth make it impossible for an agency or youth serving clinician to avoid confronting the many clinical issues, risks and expenses associated with the treatment of these youth. Residential treatment centers, foster home networks, outpatient clinics, adult and juvenile correctional facilities are increasingly challenged to provide service to aggressive and violent youth.

For many private not for profit agencies, the development of treatment programming to meet the needs of these youth is not only a clinical necessity, but a fact of survival as well. Youth who were once referred to treatment in residential and other out of home placements such as hospitals are increasingly being treated in the community. As a result, those youth that now form the basis for referrals into such settings are the very ones whose violent and aggressive behaviors once caused them to be rejected for treatment. Now, in today's managed care environment, agencies no longer have the luxury of such a choice. These youth must be taken into treatment. To survive, agencies must develop intervention programs that are both clinically effective and cost effective.

In addition, often when taken into clinical settings, even as a diversion from the justice system, many of these youth actively resist involvement in treatment programming. When these youth are engaged in treatment, the traditional methods of intervention are either inappropriate or ineffective. The result of this dynamic is that staff members become frustrated, angry and develop strong feelings of resignation and powerlessness. When this happens, the youth is either released from treatment, categorized as hopeless or eventually sent to the juvenile or adult correctional system. When these youth enter a correctional system, they pose new challenges and increasingly difficult problems for this setting. Such youth bring a depth of emotional and behavioral dysfunction for which both the adult and juvenile justice systems are ill-equipped.

Consequently, as the numbers of these violent and resistive youth in treatment and correctional settings continues to increase the resources of both the counselors and the agencies become severely taxed, even overwhelmed. These youth bring with them violence, self-mutilating behaviors, poor impulse control, oppositional and negativistic behaviors as well as highly dysfunctional family backgrounds. Family and community support is often limited or totally lacking.

As well, agencies are challenged in today's clinical environment to treat these youth more quickly, in problem focused manner and to avoid, whenever possible, any type of residential or institutional placement. But at the same time, counselors and agencies are held increasingly accountable for issues of liability and safety of release into the community. Faced with these ever increasing problems, shrinking resources and increased fiscal and legal accountability, it is no surprise that both counselors and agency administrators feel ill prepared and overwhelmed.

The purpose of this book is to assist clinicians in adult and juvenile mental health treatment and correctional settings to develop and implement effective systems of care for aggressive youth. This is a book written by a practicing clinician for other clinicians that work with violent and aggressive youth. The concepts and approaches are drawn from the research data on these youth as from the author's experience in youth intensive treatment facilities, juvenile correctional institutions, adult prisons and in forensic, maximum security psychiatric settings.

This book will outline a model that is designed for practical and functional assessment, treatment planning and service delivery to aggressive youth. In addition, since many of these youth are resistant or unwilling to enter into treatment voluntarily, another focus will be on strategies for engagement into treatment of "unwilling youth." Given the increased fiscal and legal accountability confronting clinicians, this book will also address issues of risk assessment, malpractice, liability and release risk analysis. It also provides a framework for treatment that has been applied successfully with individuals in a number of settings and programmatically in a number of facilities. The author has successfully utilized these approaches in a private residential setting for youth, community based youth mental health programs, in a prison residential treatment unit, community based settings and in a publicly funded maximum-security psychiatric hospital.

While the initial portions of this book present statistical and research data as well as developmental concepts, its purpose is not to be a theoretical compilation of current findings or a textbook of human development. Neither does this book address the larger, social policy concerns raised by the problem of violent youth in our society. These considerations are, of course, vital to the overall solution of the problem of violence in our society. There remains, always, the daily dilemmas faced by clinicians who have chose (or have been chosen) to attempt to treat aggressive youth. Thus, in this work, models of development and research data are presented as a framework for and a grounding of clinical interventions with violent youth. The focus of this work, then, is upon the practical and the applied needs of the therapist who confronts the demands and needs of violent youth.

As our discussion begins, it is important to keep in mind the words of Harry Stack Sullivan, who once said: *"Beyond all else, we are more simply human than otherwise."* We are, after all, more alike than different.

Chapter 1

The Problem of Violence in Our Society

Sometimes it seems from even a casual look at the newspapers that aggression and violence are perhaps the most common, or one of the most common forms of interaction between individuals. We daily encounter stories of assault, random violence, and other attacks on persons. It appears as if we live in a world which is increasingly terrifying and out of control. In the television and newspapers, we learn of youth that, just released from a treatment setting, commit some horrifically violent act. Other youth, for no apparent reason, seemingly erupt and seriously injure or kill someone. Efforts at "rehabilitation" are nearly unanimously decried as having failed. Even many mental health and social service professionals publicly report that these violent, antisocial youth are beyond any help and can only be removed from the community.

In response, many locales and states have become far more restrictive when dealing with these youth. Aggressive and antisocial youth are now sent to juvenile correctional facilities at an earlier age and often for much longer periods of time. A substantial number of youth are now serving time in adult correctional facilities. In fact, it will not be long, according to trends in correctional populations, that there will be more youth incarcerated in adult facilities than in juvenile correctional institutions. Although recent crime statistics from the United States Department of Justice (1996) suggest a recent drop in the number of violent crimes reported, this is, for treatment providers, a misleading statistic. Many of the perpetrators of violent crimes are now either incarcerated in adult or juvenile correctional facilities. They will, someday, be discharged. If they do not receive proper interventions while incarcerated, then when they do leave, they will be at least as, and most likely more, violent than when they entered the system.

Violent crime has been on the rise in the United States for the past decade. Although the most recent arrest rate statistics, such as those for 1995, show a slight drop of 2.9 percent, the overall rate of violent youth adjudicated in juvenile courts since 1986 has risen by 31 percent. 23,305 Americans were estimated to have been murdered in 1994, a rate around which homicides have hovered for the past few years. Homicide is listed as the tenth leading cause of death in the United States and is the most common cause of death for African-American youth. African-American females are four times more likely to die by homicide than non African-American females and an African-American male is eleven times more likely to be murdered than a non-African-American. For babies born in the United States, the estimated lifetime probability for being a homicide victim ranged from 1 in 496 for a white female baby to 1 in 27 for a black male baby.

There were 102,096 forcible rates reported to law enforcement in 1994 and an estimated total of 1.1 million aggravated assaults were also reported. While these statistics reflect a slight drop in 1994 the overall trend for the past thirty years has been consistently upward. To illustrate, between 1965 and 1992, the number of reported violent crimes increased by 432 percent. Between 1983 to 1992, the number of reported violent crimes increased by 52 percent. Thus, the most recent 1994 drop must be seen with considerable caution. As noted by FBI director Louis J. Fresh in November 1995, "the ominous increase in juvenile crime coupled with population trends portend future crime and violence at nearly unprecedented levels."

During a 100 hour period in our streets, we lose three times as many young men as we did during 100 hours in the Persian Gulf ground war. During the Gulf air war, twenty-four Americans were killed in action, during the same period, there were fifty-two homicides in Dallas. An estimated 40 percent of all traumatic spine injuries in Detroit result from gunshot wounds. The overall cost of violence, counting both the treatment of victims and the criminal justice response to the perpetrators is now estimated at over 60 billion dollars annually.

Between the years of 1984 and 1995, the number of men and women in jails and prisons in the United States nearly doubled. Felony arrest rates for violent crimes soared 37 percent between 1985 and 1989. In 1995, the United States Justice Department reported that 1.6 million Americans are currently incarcerated. By the end of 1995,

1 out of every 167 Americans was either in a prison or a jail, compared to 1 out of every 320 in 1985. The rate of incarceration has risen from 313 youth per 100,000 citizens to 600 per 100,000 in 1995. This is the highest rate of incarceration in the world. As of December 1995, there were 1,078,357 men and women in federal and state prisons, which represented and 8.7 percent increase over the previous year.

THE PROBLEM OF JUVENILE VIOLENCE

Regarding the involvement of juveniles in violent crime, the National Criminal Justice Reference Service (1995) reported that the 19 percent of the increase in violent crime between 1983 and 1992 could be attributed to juveniles. In 1992, 12.8 (or 1 in 8) of all violent crimes were cleared by the arrest of a juvenile. In contrast, in the period between 1974 and 1983, juveniles were far less responsible for the 30 percent growth in violent crime seen during that time period. In fact, juvenile responsibility reached its lowest level in 1987 but has climbed steadily ever since. Between the mid 1960's and the late 1980s the proportion of murders committed by juveniles remained fairly constant between 4.5 percent and 6.0 percent. However, in 1988, the proportion rose to 6.5 percent up to 9.0 percent in 1992 and continued upward through 1994. Similar increases have been seen in the rates of juvenile involvement in other violent crimes such as robbery, forcible rape and aggravated assault.

The most recent data from the National Criminal Justice Reference Service indicates that since 1980, the number of juvenile homicide offenders has nearly doubled and the vast majority has been age fifteen or older. The FBI Supplemental Homicide Reports for 1984 though 1991 indicate that the largest increases in juvenile homicides can be found among minority males using handguns to kill acquaintances (generally other minority youth). Juvenile homicides in the course of other crimes increased over 200 percent, while homicides precipitated by an interpersonal conflict increased by 83 percent. In comparison with adults, juvenile homicide offenders are far more likely to utilize a handgun in the commission of a murder.

The juvenile violent crime arrest rate in the United States reached its highest level ever: 514 arrests per 100, 000 youth age ten through seventeen. From 1975 through 1988, the juvenile arrest rates for violent crimes remained relatively constant, but have climbed rapidly in the past few years. Specifically, the rate of arrests of juveniles per 100,000 (ages ten through seventeen) stood at slightly above 300 in 1975 and 1985 but climbed above 400 in 1991 and above 500 in 1993.

Of the 2.7 million arrests of persons under the age of eighteen arrested in 1994, over 150,000 were for violent crimes (murder, rape, robbery, and aggravated assault) and nearly 160,000 arrests for drug abuse violations. Also in 1994, nearly one in fivearrests for violent offenses was of a juvenile. It is interesting to note that the statistics suggest a growing and extremely significant violent subgroup of juveniles. Although the juvenile violent offense rate rose 54 percent between 1988 and 1994, less than one half of one percent of juveniles (about 1 in every 200) was arrested for a violent crime in 1994.

Between 1984 and 1994, the number of juvenile murderers known to police tripled. In 1994, some 2800 juveniles were responsible for killing an estimated 2300 people. This is more than two and one half times the number of persons killed by juveniles in 1984. Eight in ten juveniles who killed used a gun, compared to five in ten in 1984. Overall, between 1984 and 1994, four times as many juveniles killed with a gun. Murders by juveniles acting alone and juveniles acting with others in groups have both increased substantially since 1984. More than half of the juveniles who killed did so with an accomplice and 30 percent of those accomplices were adults. In 1993, almost half of all high school students reported weapons in their schools and about 40 percent reported gangs.

THE MISPERCEPTION OF THE DECLINE IN JUVENILE CRIME

There is another factor which must be accounted for in the well publicized recent decline in juvenile crimes: the number of youth held in custody in private and public facilities in the United States is at record levels and shows an increasing trend. While the population of youth in the United States declined by 11 percent between 1979 and 1989, the number of juveniles in custody increased by 31 percent and the overall custody rates for juveniles in public and private juvenile facilities increased by 46 percent from 251 per 100,000 in 1979 to 367 per 100,000 in 1989. The rate of custody for private facilities increased 48 percent while the custody rate for public facilities increased 45 percent (United States Department of Justice, 1992). In 1991, 36,190 youth were place in 1,032 private facilities and 57,542 juveniles were held in 1076 public facilities. This was the largest population of juveniles in public facilities since the census began in 1974. These figures represent a 2.5 percent increase over 1989 in the number of juveniles held while the number of facilities has decreased by 2 percent. Thus, more youth are being held in fewer places. This population increase is further characterized by a trend setting rise in the number of youth held for violent offenses.

Of the youth held in public facilities, 95 percent of them are held for crimes that would be considered criminal if committed by adults. Further, many states have lowered the age at which a juvenile may be transferred to the jurisdiction of the adult courts and subsequently sent to an adult correctional facility. In 1995, an estimated 7,888 youth were held in adult jails, a 17 percent increase over the previous year. More than 75 percent of these youth had either been tried as an adult or were awaiting bind-over.

While at first look, the recent drop in juvenile crime rates may seem encouraging, any enthusiasm must be tempered by the sobering fact that many more youth are being held in custody today and are generally being held for longer periods of time. It may not be that intervention efforts have started to reduce the amount of juvenile crime. It may simply be that because more youth are incarcerated for longer periods of time, the number of youth in the community who commit crimes has been reduced. This, of course, is a temporary and artificial solution. Youth are released from correctional facilities. Even if youth are committed for longer periods of time, those commitments will end. And the youth released from settings without treatment programs will surely be far more violent and criminal than those who were in settings with treatment programs.

Because of this increased trend in violence, those youth seen by counselors and clinicians in community and residential treatment centers are increasingly violent, resistive and aggressive, This next chapter will discuss current research findings concerning this challenging clinical population.

Chapter 2

The Problem of Violence
in Mental Health Treatment

Because of the increasing rates of violent crime, the violent client in treatment programs now represents a significant, often highly visible subgroup in both adult and juvenile settings. Although the numbers of incarcerated violent youth has increased substantially, currently, more is known about violence committed by adults than by youth.

It is known that youth in correctional treatment settings are increasingly violent and show increasing evidence of severe psychological problems. Aggressive youth who were once only confined in specialized, highly secure facilities are now being treated in non-secure hospitals, residential treatment centers and community settings. A number of efforts, including the federally funded CASPP program and the Alaska Youth Initiative have designed promising interventions to keep violent youth in community programs. However, such programs are not always successful. Only when such programs fail, is a youth generally placed in a private residential facility or a public institution. Increasingly, then, in order to be admitted to a residential public or private facility, the youth must have actually committed an act of violence.

Placement in institutions is quite expensive. Public agencies such as the courts and child welfare agencies face the dilemma of increasing numbers of seriously disturbed youth and decreasing financial resources to pay the treatment. Due to these funding limitations, many placing agencies are quite reluctant to put all but the most severely disturbed youth in a residential setting. These circumstances have caused a number of shifts in the service delivery system. First of all, many youth that were once placed in institutions or residential programs because of their behaviors must now be treated in the community. Staff members of these community agencies are often ill prepared to address the complex and turbulent needs of violent youth.

If a youth cannot be successfully managed in the community, the next treatment option is some type of residential setting. These are generally foster home networks, group homes, halfway houses or residential treatment centers. These programs once did not take these youth, feeling that their "acting-out," "anti-social," or "delinquent" behavior made them inappropriate for the "therapeutic milieu." However, now, to financially survive, treatment centers have been forced to take who were once rejected for admission as "untreatable." Now, these very youth may now be the primary youth group of these agencies. To further complicate matters, the wide spread uses of "managed care" approach forces agencies to treat these youth in less time with less expensive resources. It is not uncommon for a residential facility to have had a one-year average length of stay to now see that average drop to below ninety days. Secure, intensive treatment facilities have typically even less time available to them, often less than thirty days.

Paradoxically, as the demands upon agencies to treat these youth have grown, the knowledge base about them has not. Very little is known about violent youth. Much more, as is typically the case, is known about violent adult mentally disordered clients. Since violence is generally seen as a developmental phenomenon, a review of current data concerning adult clients can conceivably help in the understanding of both adult and juvenile violent clients in treatment and correctional settings.

THE VIOLENT ADULT PSYCHIATRIC PATIENT

In regards to the greater body of knowledge concerning the adult client, earlier research suggested that the rate of violence by psychiatric patients was below that for the general population. Recent data suggests that while this is true for patients who have never been hospitalized, those persons who have been hospitalized in public hospitals under the dangerousness standards actually have a higher rate of violence.

Two recent large-scale community epidemiological studies have demonstrated that, according to Borum (1996) certain symptoms of mental illness may be, in fact, a significant predictor of violent behavior. Swanson et al. (1990) using violence specific questions embedded within the clinical interview found a higher rate of violence among psychiatric patients in three large metropolitan areas. Link, Andrews and Cullen (1992) compared mental patients and never treated community residents from a high crime area of New York City using a variety of official and self-report measures. Psychiatric patients were found to have higher rates on all measures of violent/illegal behavior. These behaviors could not be accounted for by sociodemographic and/or community context variables. A scale of psychotic symptoms (the false beliefs and perceptions scale from the Psychiatric Epidemiology Research Interview as well as thirteen items such as feeling possessed, feeling thoughts were not one's own, and beliefs of mind control) was the only variable which accounted for the difference in violent behavior.

Circincione et al. (1992) reported that in a 1978 cohort of adult males admitted to a state mental health facility that a diagnosis of schizophrenia was a significant predictor of violent arrests. For patients with no prior arrests, diagnosis was not a significant predictor. Thus, adult males with schizophrenia with a prior arrest history are at greater risk.

A recent study by Tardiff (1997) studied the rates and patterns of violence toward persons by psychiatric patients before admission to an inpatient service of the Payne Whitney Clinic and determined which factors were associated with a greater risk of violence. The patterns of violence were similar for men and women in terms of target severity of injuries, use of a weapon, and place of occurrence. Univariate analyses showed that only youth was associated with violence for male patients, while youth, low socioeconomic status, substance abuse, and Axis II pathology were associated with a greater risk of violence for female patients. The frequency of violence by female patients was 150 percent higher than it was in a study at the Payne Whitney Clinic a decade ago. The frequency of violence by male patients was 50 percent higher than it was a decade ago. In the current study, substance abuse was associated with greater risk of violence by patients.

Heilbrun (1993) in a comprehensive review of violent behavior and psychiatric diagnosis reports the presence of Obsessive Compulsive Disorder, Panic Disorder, Major Depression, Major Depression with Grief, Bipolar Disorder or Schizophrenia or Schizophreniform Disorder raises the frequency of violent behavior from 2 percent to 12 percent. The presence of substance abuse raises it further to 19 percent. The presence of two or more diagnoses approximately doubles the risk of violence (Swanson, 1990). The highest risk for violence was found in persons with the presence of schizophrenia or affective disorder plus substance abuse. Link (1992) found that a history of treatment for a mental disorder increases the incidence of aggression on an average of 1.5 to 4 times over that of a never treated person in the community.

The most recent and definitive study to date (Steadman, 1998) found that patients who were discharged from psychiatric facilities who did not abuse alcohol or illegal drugs had a rate of violence no different than their neighbors in the community. However, substance abuse raised the rate of violence among both psychiatric patients and non-patients.

THE INCREASING SEVERITY OF EMOTIONAL PROBLEMS OF VIOLENT YOUTH IN CORRECTIONS

As little as is known about the treatment of adults, even less is known about the mental health needs of violent youth. The knowledge base concerning the mental health needs of youth has, historically, been limited. As stated by Otto et al. (1992), a review of the past thirty years of research literature addressing the mental health needs of youth with mental disorders in the juvenile justice system has been given scant attention. This lack of knowledge about the extent of the problem parallels that of the adult system. It is generally understood, however, that youth in the juvenile justice system have seriously unmet mental health needs.

What research that does exist indicates that youth held in correctional facilities exhibit significant emotional problems and are more similar than dissimilar to youth in psychiatric treatment settings, with aggression being the major discriminating variable for confinement Davis et al. (1991).

Otto (1992) in a review of the research concerning the prevalence of emotional disorder in the juvenile justice system reported that while the general population prevalence rate for mental disorders among youth ranges to a high of 22 percent, the rate of mental disorder in the juvenile justice samples was considerably higher. Typically, between 20 percent and 60 percent of incarcerated youth were found to have a conduct disorder. The rate of psychotic disorders was found to range between 1 percent and 6 percent, a rate higher than the general population. Attention deficit disorders and mood disorders were found to be a significant problem for incarcerated youth.

To illustrate, Davis (1991) studied a 10 percent random sample of youth incarcerated in the Ohio Department of Youth Services. This study utilized a variety of measures including record review, standardized measures such as the Revised Problem Behavior Checklist, Children's Brief Psychiatric Rating Scale and Clinical Interview by psychiatrists and psychologists. The data indicated a 32 percent prevalence rate of major affective disorders, with a significant subpopulation (21 percent) evidencing symptoms of depression prior to incarceration. As was reflected in other data, a significant number of youth (66 percent) had a history of substance abuse. Forty-six percent of the youth reported a history of alcohol abuse. Nineteen percent were found to exhibit Attention Deficit Hyperactivity Disorder, 17 percent were seen as evidencing a developing personality disorder or were given personality disorder diagnoses. Another 17 percent were seen as having learning disabilities and 6 percent were given a diagnosis of anxiety disorder. These youth evidenced a high rate of suicidal ideation and behavior. 14 percent displayed active suicidal behavior during the time of the study and 21 percent reported suicidal threats in the past. Nearly 20 percent had at least one psychiatric hospitalization prior to incarceration. Many youth were found to have multiple diagnoses.

Most of the prevalence studies concerning incarcerated youth have not explored the issue of posttraumatic stress disorder. This is primarily due to the time in which the research took place. At those times, the level of awareness of the problem was not known, although many studies reported a history of physical and sexual abuse (Davis, 1991). Clearly, as more incarcerated youth are assessed with the criteria for post traumatic stress disorder, the prevalence rate of this disorder will likely increase.

VIOLENCE IN TREATMENT SETTINGS

Staff members who are victimized in treatment settings themselves suffer psychological consequences. In a study of youth workers assaulted on the job, Snow (1994) found that through use of a semi-structured interview, many staff met the diagnostic criteria for Posttraumatic Stress Disorder (PTSD). All of the staff had been physically assaulted. As well, the youth had hit the staff with weapons or thrown them at the staff. Ninety percent of the staff had felt fearful that they were at risk of physical danger at work. They experienced psychological distress (reexperiencing of trauma, avoiding or numbing of responsiveness, and increased arousal) as a result of their youth assaultive behavior. Sixty percent of the staff reported increased alcohol intake and 25 percent of subjects increased drug use following the incidents. Lastly, it was noted 65 percent of the staff noted that there were few supports available to them following an assault.

A NEW PARADIGM FOR TREATMENT
OF VIOLENT YOUTH

The change to increasingly violent treatment populations requires that youth serving agencies develop new models of treatment, as well as to modify current approaches. The treatment paradigm outlined in this book utilizes developmental perspectives of Patterson (1989), Erikson (1959), and Piaget (1963) together with the model of violent behavior of Monahan (1981). This theory suggests four primary psychological domains of cognitive processes, affective reactions, behavioral responses and social-environmental influences and was drawn from the Novaco (1975) conceptualization of anger arousal. These theoretical approaches as well as the social-cognitive model of anger and aggression of Lochman (1991) form the conceptual basis for cognitive-behavioral-expressive interventions (Davis and Boster, 1987; Davis and Boster, 1988) with aggressive youth. This model was developed from interventions with a maximum-security forensic psychiatric population and has been successfully applied to youth in residential settings and to youth treated in community settings.

This model places its emphasis upon the developmental characteristics of aggressive youth. As well, it is multimodal in nature, using various avenues of interaction with the youth. To illustrate, since many aggressive youth have been found to have verbal information processing deficits, the use of creative art therapy allows learning through the visual rather than verbal channels of learning.

Further, as will be detailed later, it is known that violent behavior does not have one single cause. Rather, violent behavior arises from a variety of influences. Such influences can include early trauma, exposure to violent role models, biochemical factors, and sociological factors, and certain types of mental and neurological disorders as well as substance abuse. Because the origins of violence are many, the concept that only one approach or model will successfully treat the problem of violence is an illusionary parsimony. That is to say, we are simply fooling ourselves if we think that the complex problem of youth's violence can have a simple solution. Rather, we must look at interventions which address the multiple pathways to violent behavior (Pepler and Slaby, 1994; Cornell, 1990).

For this reason, we shall first address a model of human development that is, itself, multifactorial in nature. After the general understanding of this model is put forth in the next chapter, we will then apply it to what is known about violent seriously emotionally disabled youth.

Chapter 3

Developmental Sequences Utilizing a Cognitive-Behavioral Expressive Model

Human development is multifactorial in nature. Complex behaviors such as aggression are multi-causal in origin. Resultantly, a multifaceted model of development is required to understand the nature of violent behavior in youth. Treatment interventions should be based upon the developmental level of the youth or youth in treatment. This is needed because youth at varying developmental stages think, feel and act in different ways. A youth who is developmentally unable to think in abstract terms will have great difficulty understanding abstract concepts such as relative justice or higher moral principles. Instead, the non-abstract thinking young person will look at a situation in simplistic, "either-or" fashion. Rather than understanding that "justice" requires more than simple retribution, the aggressive youth is much more likely to see things in terms of an "eye for an eye." Often, aggression is described as a "problem solving behavior." Yet, if the youth is not developmentally (as a result of any number of personological or environmental factors) capable of solving higher level conceptual problems, how can we expect an intervention based on such a premise to be successful. It is far more effective to attempt to determine where the aggressive youth's functions developmentally and then develop interventions that assist in his or her growth or development in a healthy, nonviolent manner.

The model by which aggressive youth are to be understood is a combination of a variety of developmental theories condensed into four primary domains, or areas, of functioning. These domains are cognitive, affective (or emotional), behavioral/motor and social-environmental.

In Table 3.1, this model is portrayed. Across the top, the cognitive developmental sequences of Piaget are listed under the cognitive domain, together with Kohlberg's (1976) stages of moral development. In the affective domain, the gradual differentiation of emotions as first suggested by Bridges (1933) is portrayed. Behavioral development follows the gradients of Gesell (1954) and the psychosocial developmental model of Erikson (1959) is described under the social-environmental domains.

GENERAL CONCEPTS OF DEVELOPMENT

Each of these four larger domains, of course, has sub-domains or influences. As well, the domains interact with each other in a cybernetic fashion. For example social-environmental factors as well as neurochemical toxins can substantially influence cognitive development. Or, to use another illustration, affective functioning can be considerably influenced by the biochemistry of the individual's brain, such as serotonin levels as well as social role modeling. Thus, rather than attempting to establish a single, underlying cause of violence, this model attempts to explain violent behavior of youth in four global areas of adaptation to the environment.

The term, "adaptation," is vital to the understanding of violence. Violence is a type of interaction between the youth and part of the environment of those youth. From the moment of our birth, we adapt and change to the demands of the world surrounding us. How we adapt is determined both by what dispositional factors we bring with us (for example, genetic pre-dispositions) and what environmental factors (such as the nature of our social world) shape us.

Another important concept in development is the nature of the changes that result as the person interacts with the environment. Change can be quantitative, that is, how much or how less of a factor results from an interaction. To illustrate, the verbal development of a child can be quantitatively described by counting how many words a child of a certain age can correctly identify. In reference to violence, the number of violent thoughts can be counted in both aggressive and non-aggressive children.

TABLE 3.1. Developmental Matrix

AGE	COGNITIVE	AFFECTIVE	BEHAVIORAL	SOCIAL
0-2	Sensorimotor Egocentric	Primitive Unorganized	Reflexive Reactive	Trust versus mistrust
2-5	Preoperational thought Development of symbolic play Pre-conventional mortality	Dyscontrolled Global	Gross motor locomotion Parallel Play	Autonomy versus shame and doubt
5-12	Concrete operational thought Nonabstract problem solving Conventional mortality	Narrow band of emotions Impulsive Stereotypical emotional expression	Cognitively mediated behavior Fine motor skills development	Industry versus inferiority Social Play
12-Adult	Formal operations Flexibility Universal ethical principle	Broad band of emotional expression Specificity Responsive	Development of assertive behavior Complex motor skill development	Indentity versus role diffusion Social skills differentiation and refinement

Change can also be qualitative, that is a change in the process, function or nature of a certain behavior or aspect of an individual. Returning to the example of verbal development, a qualitative difference can be found in the types of ideas expressed by the words of a child. For example, an older child not only knows more words than a younger child but also is better able to understand more abstract concepts such as fair play.

In the discussion of the development of violent youth, both quantitative and qualitative differences in each of the four domains are important. They cannot be confused with each other, especially in the area of treatment. To illustrate, just because an youth can, by rote memory, name a number of non-violent behaviors, this does not mean that the youth will be able to actually apply that list to his or her life. Listing is a concrete, quantitative action. Application involves a qualitative change in how one responds to a specific circumstance. Having an youth learn stock phrases such as "just say no" to aggression does not prepare him or her to actually know how to respond in a different manner. To use an example from athletics, I may very well be able to list off the various defenses used by a football team. However, memorizing the list does not mean that I will, at the proper strategic time, be able to choose the correct defensive formation to stop my opponent from scoring.

Development across the four domains is not always equal. A child may develop physically to a far more advanced extent than he or she develops cognitively. The youth who looks physically mature may not be able to reason at a mature level. If we see an youth functioning at a high level in one area of development, we cannot assume that he or she is at the same level in all other areas of development. Although a youth might sufficiently tall to grasp the steering wheel of a car and touch the pedals, this is no guarantee that he or she is mature enough to drive in a safe and responsible manner.

Turning from normal development to youth that have impediments to healthy growth, a developmental perspective becomes even more important. This is especially true, as we have learned that many aggressive youth are, themselves, the victims of physical violence. The experience of traumas such as child abuse are pervasive across many areas of functioning and may result in the victimized youth being unable to progress past a certain developmental point. A sexually victimized child, for example, may be unable to resolve basic questions of social development such as "Who can I trust and who should I not."

Instead, the youth that is a victim of physical abuse, understandably, approaches all persons as potentially harmful and threatening. This way of responding is effective in the abusive environment of the youth. In fact, for the child in an abusive environment, it would be foolish, maladaptive and potentially fatal to see things in any other way. If a youth has only experienced a violent environment, then the youth has not learned to understand that all environments, thankfully, are not as abusive as the one that he or she now inhabits. This means, of course, that if you take abused children out of the abusive environment and put them in a safe place, they will not immediately relax their guard. Rather, they may become even more guarded because newness is threatening. They may become even more distrustful and frightened, even when there is no outward reason to be that way. In this manner, what was an adaptive and helpful response in one environment becomes maladaptive and counter-productive in another environment. Thus, it is not so much that the aggressive child has something "wrong" with him or her. Instead, the child has not learned alternative ways to meet what are likely underlying healthy and "normal" needs. The following case illustration may serve to illustrate this point.

The Case of Emily: Extreme Sexualization at Age Four

Emily is a four and one half-year-old girl who was repeatedly sexually abused by her stepfather. The abuse was primary that of vaginal penetration by the stepfather with his penis. Apparently, the abuse lasted for nearly two years. Another adult family member discovered it when the perpetrator was in the act of abusing Emily. The stepfather was incarcerated and Emily was placed in a foster home. There, she was observed to masturbate openly and to such a frequency that the behavior had a compulsive quality. She would touch the other child in the home in his genitalia and would often expose herself. She was unable to sleep through the night, was easily startled and frightened, and had frequent nightmares.

She was referred for a mental health assessment and treatment of what was seen as Posttraumatic Stress Disorder due to her sexual victimization. During the first appointment, she was taken into a play therapy room that had a number of dolls and other toys. She sat on the floor, across the room from the therapist and began to play with the dolls. Then, after a few minutes, she looked up at the male therapist, pulled her dress up and asked, "Want to screw?" The therapist explained that adults should not do such things with children. She became visibly anxious and began to touch her genital area.

Emily, clearly, knew of no other way to relate to an adult male. As is typical of many sexually abused children, her social behavior developed in a highly sexualized manner. She inappropriately touched other children. She compulsively masturbated to relieve her anxiety. She knew of only way to relate to an adult male (or perhaps acted in this manner to fend off a perceived threat). If untreated, of course, such tragic victims develop into adults who have severe impairment in their sexual and social functioning.
In the chapters that follow, each of the following domains are described in terms of how they specifically relate to aggression and violence in youth. The reader is referred to the original sources for a more detailed explanation of the theories here presented in an overview format. The next chapter will discuss how violent youth seem to follow a "pathway" in the development of antisocial behavior.

Chapter 4

Pathways of Violent Youth

THE DEVELOPMENTAL PATHWAY MODEL

In recent years, a new understanding of aggressive behaviors has emerged using a developmental pathway model. Much of this new view can be credited to the work of Gerald Patterson and his colleagues. Rather than seeing aggression as a behavior that suddenly happens or is a reaction to a circumstance, violence is seen as a pattern of behavior characteristic of the child. Aggressive behavior is a pattern that emerges at an early age. Without intervention, violence remains an enduring characteristic of the person. It appears to be a developmental trait that begins early in life and often continues into adolescence and adulthood. For many youth, stable manifestations of antisocial behavior begin as early as preelementary school grades.

A significant body of research by Patterson and his colleagues (1989) suggests an "early starter model" which describes a family matrix that directly trains youth in antisocial behavior. It is suggested that the family directly reinforce the aggressive and antisocial behavior of the child. These antisocial behaviors then transfer from the home to other settings and then lead to social failures. The end result of this process is an enduring pattern of antisocial and aggressive behavior. Patterson (1989) suggests that antisocial behavior seen at grade 4 is predictive of later aggressive behavior. A number of developmental variables have been consistently identified as covariates for aggression in both youth and adults. As indicated by Patterson, families of aggressive youth are characterized by harsh and inconsistent discipline, and aggressive individuals are frequently the victims of physical abuse as children. Parents tend to be socially unskilled and inept, so that the child learns to manipulate or coerce others instead of learning appropriate social skills. Although some parents may positively reinforce aggressive behavior, escape/avoidance is often the primary factor; the child uses aversive behavior to terminate aversive intrusions by family members, that is, the child acts obnoxiously to force others to leave him or her alone. As the pattern continues, the parents escalate their coercion to hitting and physical attacks, and thus the child learns that aggression can be used to control others. This pattern of aggression leads to rejection by the peer group, not the reverse, and results in either deviant peer group membership or social isolation.

Rejected aggressive youth are deficient in a number of pro-social skills including positive peer group entry, perception of peer group norms, and response to provocation and interpretation of pro-social interactions. Family stresses such as substance abuse, poverty, divorce, and domestic violence are equally associated with violent youth. There is a high degree of intergenerational similarity for antisocial behavior. Having one antisocial, aggressive parent places a child at significant risk for aggressive behavior, with an even higher risk when both parents are antisocial. Patterson has documented concordance across three generations.

The Case of Jim: A Father and Son Crime Team

Jim is a 16-year-old youth who is currently confined in a state juvenile correctional facility on a charge of burglary. This is his first incarceration, but both his father and his grandfather have prison records. He reports that two cousins and an uncle are currently confined in the adult correctional system.

Jim's father was a professional burglar. He brought Jim up in the "family business." Beginning in elementary school, Jim was taught by his father on how to be a thief. He learned what types of houses were likely targets. He learned how to identify alarm systems and to disable them. Eventually, he would ride along with his father and soon began to enter the house with his father. His father continued to teach him the skills of being a burglar. For example, he taught Jim to never carry a weapon, because in their state, arrest with a gun added a mandatory three years onto the sentence. He was also taught to never use stolen credit cards because, with today's computers, the numbers of the stolen cards could be quickly transmitted and alert store security.

When his father got older, Jim took over the building entry portion of the "business." His father "fenced" the stolen items. Jim eventually met a girl, a runaway. She moved in with him. One morning, Jim returned from a successful night of burglary. Being quite tired, he went straight to bed. His new girlfriend woke up shortly after that and saw the loot spread about the living room. Mixed in with other items was a purse, and in that purse were credit cards. She took them and went on a shopping spree. Much as Jim's father had predicted, the cards had already been called in. She was apprehended by store security trying to buy some clothing with one of the cards. When taken down to police headquarters, she quickly implicated Jim.

After Jim was arrested and sent to the correctional institution, his father visited him. Jim later related that the primary point of his father's visit was to assure that Jim had learned this hard but valuable lesson about trusting girlfriends.

Quinn (1995) to illustrate further found that there are critical factors that identified those 1st grade boys who were at risk for developing antisocial behavior. These factors were higher teacher ratings of aggression, more negative peer interactions on the playground and lower levels of academic-engaged time than were their comparison peers.

Stability coefficients for childhood aggression challenge those of intelligence quotients. Early behaviors such as temper tantrums and grade school troublesomeness have been found to significantly predict youth and adult offenses, and suggest an underlying developmental continuum. Nursery school children who obtain goals through aggression are likely to go on using this behavior to pursue such goals. Longitudinal studies of both Swedish and American youth show a clear pattern of aggression beginning in preschool and continuing to adulthood. The studies reveal one group of chronically aggressive youth and another group of chronic victims. The aggressive behavior of the youth was consistent and evident as much as fifteen years later.

As can be seen from the preceding case study, how one learns to view the world and the cognitive patterns that are learned seem to have a great deal to do with later behavior. The next chapter shall focus specifically upon the development of cognitive processes in aggressive youth and young adults.

Chapter 5

General Principles
of Cognitive Development

The renowned developmental psychologist, Jean Piaget formulated a model of cognitive growth that has become a landmark in developmental psychology. Piaget observed the development of his two nieces as they learned about their world and detailed his findings in his 1963 text, *The Origins of Intelligence in Children*, Piaget stated that human cognitive development builds from the simple to the complex. Development involves a continuous process of change and adaptation in the manner in which we deal with our environment. Development is the result of four factors, *maturation, experience, social transmission,* and the process of *equilibrium. Maturation* is the unfolding of the genetic blueprints in our life. *Experience* refers to the active process of interaction between the child and the environment. *Social transmission* describes the information and customs passed along from parents and other persons in the environment to the child. Lastly, the process of *Equilibrium* describes the nature of human development. The growing child seeks to maintain a balance between what he or she knows and what he or she is experiencing.

In this process of development, there are discreet stages of cognitive change. These stages are hierarchical and discreet. The process of thought in each stage is qualitatively and quantitatively different from the other. As well, to progress to a higher stage, one must move through all of the proceeding stages of thought. Thus, one cannot move from the first to the last stage without passing through all those that lie in between.

As the child develops, he or she creates cognitive *schemes,* or methods of dealing with the environment which can be generalized to many situations. To illustrate, an abused child will frequently develop a scheme of the world as a hostile and dangerous place. Thus, each time the child views a new situation, he or she views it as potentially threatening and harmful. Or as another example, racial prejudice could be partially understood as the application of a fixed schema to all persons who have specific characteristics.

When a child takes in the environment, he or she must *adapt* or adjust to the environment in order to survive. Adaptation involves two processes that complement each other: *assimilation* and *accommodation*. *Assimilation* takes place when newly learned information is altered to fit existing patterns of thought. For example, the young child may describe all men as "Daddy." As another illustration, it may be known by some that there was once a requirement that all graduate students drive a beat up Volkswagen beetle. I was no exception and my then two-year-old son knew the vehicle as "Daddy's Bug Car." Once while driving our other car, we drove past a similar Volkswagen. Josh became hysterical; believing that someone else was driving his father's "Bug Car."

This process of assimilation is not limited to just children. To continue with the Volkswagen example, these cars had a reputation as being quite easy to repair, even by a "Complete Idiot" as one celebrated repair manual claimed. For me, a Volkswagen repair should have been easy. My family, on my father's side, had a long history with the railroad. My grandfather was a railroad mechanic who rose to running the railroad roundhouse. When my father was a teen, my grandfather took him to a junkyard to find a vehicle. They then rebuilt it and my father continues to treasure the memory of his Ford "Model A." If development were strictly genetic, it would stand to reason that I, too, would be able to repair things mechanical. But try as I did, the only thing I successfully learned to do was the relatively simple act of tuning up the engine. This worked wonderfully when the problem was the lack of a tune up. Unfortunately, beyond changing the oil, it was the only thing I could do. So, when the brakes went out, I tuned the engine. Then, as I crashed into the wall because I could not stop the care, I could at least listen to the purring of that well (and frequently) tuned engine.

Accommodation takes place when one must modify existing thought patterns to fit new information. It is, in essence, a new way of thinking. Youth, who have been chronically abused, to return to this example, typically are unable to easily accommodate new social information. Rather, they will persistently and, often, illogically to an outside observer, attempt to assimilate social information into pre-existing structures. Thus, the new and well meaning youth care worker who attempts to hug a distraught abused child may be unpleasantly surprised by the child's negative and potentially violent reaction.

While each stage has approximate age ranges (as is the case with all of the domains of development) these stages are *approximate* and are best seen as guideposts. Further, as a result of trauma or some type of developmental disability or influence, a person may stay fixated within one stage and not progress to another. This is a central point in the understanding of violent behavior. Over the years, research has demonstrated that violent persons think differently than nonviolent persons. Not only do they think differently in terms of content (more violent fantasies, for example), they also think a *qualitatively* different way. As will be seen, the form of their thinking often does not allow for the more abstract concepts non violent persons use to stifle or suppress violent impulses.

Piaget's first stage, *Sensorimotor*, takes place between birth and two years of age. The infant explores the world through the senses such as sight, taste, and motor activity. During this period, the child develops *object permanence*, the understanding that people and objects do not disappear merely because they are out of sight.

The second stage *Pre-Operational* lasts from ages two through seven, approximately. They learn that one thing can symbolically stand for another. (A piece of wood can become a toy airplane, for example.) Children of this age are "magical" in their thinking at times, tending to believe that inanimate objects can become alive. Children at this age are quite egocentric, believing that each person sees the world in the same manner as he or she views it. Once, for example, when I was down with the flu, young Josh brought me his Winnie the Pooh blanket, reasoning that since it made him feel good, that it would have the same effect on me. Egocentricity can result in social difficulties. Those who need to experience something before it is learned are advised to take three two-year-olds, put them in a room and try to have them share favorite toys. As your grandmother will tell you, this is impossible. In a much more serious light, when divorce happens while a child is in this cognitive stage, it is easy to see how the child could blame himself or herself for the destruction of the family.

At approximately seven years of age, the child moves to the *Concrete Operations* stage. Here, the child becomes gradually less egocentric and develops more sophisticated processes of thought such as conservation, the recognition that a quart of water in a tall pitcher has the same mass as a quart of water in a stout container. The child's thinking remains highly concrete and full of literal interpretations. It is also known that frontal lobe brain-injured persons think in a highly concrete way. The famous Russian neuropsychologist Goldstein once reported an observation in which a brain injured patient became highly upset upon hearing a physician remark upon looking out the window during a stormy morning that "it was a dark day." To the concrete thinking patient, this was impossible. If it was dark, then it must be night. If it was day, then it could not be dark.

Finally, during adolescence (although many parents of teenagers find this hard to believe), the thinking process matures to it's highest level. The child is now able to think in a manner termed by Piaget as "Formal Operations." This most mature level of thinking results in the youth being able to deal with abstractions, test hypotheses in a mature manner and understand complex ethical issues. It is, in some sense, why youth become so concerned with matters of principals and hold to rigid absolutes. They have only begun to be able to see these issues and retain certain concrete qualities to their thinking, especially in early portions of formal operations.

A developmental psychologist, Kohlberg (1976), used Piaget's model in the concept of the development of moral reasoning. Early on in our development, we exhibit *pre-conventional* morality. All actions are seen in strict either or terms and justice is swift and sure. To illustrate, when a group of four-year-olds were asked about a young boy who had shoplifted some candy and then, on his way home, was struck by a car, the children were quite certain that the child had suffered a direct consequence to his theft. Because he had stolen, the children reasoned, being struck by a car punished him. The next stage, *Conventional Morality* is defined by an emphasis upon rules and order. If one breaks a rule, then one must be sorely punished. Justice is a matter of "an eye for an eye." There can be no room for consideration of individual or mitigating circumstances. (If one is twelve years old, therefore, one should not opt for a jury of one's peers.) Kohlberg, of course, believes that some adults have never moved out of this stage of moral reasoning. The last stage, *Universal Ethical Principal* allows for greater understanding of truths beyond mere rules of conduct. A person at this stage can understand and appreciate the civil disobedience of a Ghandi or King, for example.

Chandler and Moran (1990) studied sixty fourteen to seventeen years old male adjudicated juvenile delinquents and twenty age-matched nondelinquent controls. Each subject was administered measures of moral reasoning, social convention understanding, interpersonal awareness, socialization, empathy, autonomy, and psychopathy to explore the relations between moral reasoning, moral sentiment, and antisocial behavior. The delinquent group evidenced developmental delays on all tests of morality functioning and their performance on measures of autonomy and socialization differentiated those youth that were more or less psychopathic. Findings underscore the multidimensional character of moral development and the complexity of the relations between thought and action.

In a similar study, Trevethan and Walker (1989) examined differences in moral reasoning concerning hypothetical versus real-life conflicts of forty-four youth (aged fifteen to eighteen years) that were classified as psychopathic, delinquent, or normal. As would be expected normal youth attained a higher level of moral reasoning than either the delinquents or psychopaths. Lastly, Gibbs (1991) applied developmental and cognitive perspectives to the understanding and group treatment of antisocial youth. He suggested that a primary cause of antisocial behavior or conduct disorder is delayed sociomoral development. This is seen especially in a pattern of thinking in which the antisocial youth evidence an inordinate degree of egocentric bias and immature moral judgment. The cognitive factors that Gibbs suggests support the sociomoral developmental delay are certain cognitive distortions, especially, externalization of blame and mislabeling. For this reason, he states that not only sociomoral developmental delay but also cognitive distortion must be taken into account in treatment programs for antisocial youth.

COGNITIVE CHARACTERISTICS OF VIOLENT YOUTH

When the consideration of cognitive processes is directed at the understanding of aggression, the distinction must be drawn between the basic and essential emotion of anger and the behavioral response of violence. Anger is a basic emotion that may or may not lead to the behavior of violence. All of us feel angry, but fortunately, most of us are not violent. A large part of what determines how we respond to anger (either violently or nonviolently, for example) is how we think about or perceive the situation about which we are angry.

The way in which we think about situations is linked to the interactive mechanisms of cognitive appraisal and expectations. These are essentially learned perceptual processes. Appraisals are the characteristic way in which a person views the environment, and expectations are the person's prediction of the outcome of an anticipated behavior. Habitual appraisals and expectations predispose a person to act in a certain way in response to his or her perception of circumstances and to expect that behavior to be either successful or unsuccessful depending upon previous experiences.

COGNITIVE PROCESSES OF AGGRESSIVE YOUTH

The aggressive youth sees himself or herself as a person in a threatening world. Their past experiences of abuse and pain have taught them that. They have experienced the world to be consistently hostile and expect it to continue as such.

Studies of aggressive individuals show that even when intelligence is controlled as a factor, these persons tend to have much less developed patterns of fantasy and imagination. Aggressive children and adults have constricted imaginative resources. Persons with an active imagination are able to produce a variety of responses to situations, most of which are nonviolent and are, as well, able to consider such situations with complex, abstract reasoning. In contrast, chronically violent individuals appear to operate, in a Piagetian sense, in a concrete operational cognitive style comprising fewer available alternatives, constricted problem-solving, an inability to reason abstractly, and a focus upon violent outcomes in fantasy life.

Violent individuals appraise neutral situations in a hostile manner and have a characteristic worldview that predisposes them to aggression. The Erikson (1959) psychosocial developmental model suggests that these persons tend to retain their mistrustful worldview, most likely consequent to their early childhood experiences. They have a self-image promoting patterns of themselves as persons to be feared, seemingly to stave off strong feelings of insecurity and unresolved conflicts of inferiority. Aggressive individuals, as well, have been shown to be deficient in positive empathy toward others. Thematic Apperception Test data of violent persons have evidenced violent themes, with aggression being an expected and successful problem-solving mechanism. Violent individuals appear to be much less able to learn from aversive situations, and unable in either real life or fantasy to anticipate negative consequences of aggression. To illustrate, Guerra (1989) found that, in general, both male and female high delinquents were significantly less likely than male and female low delinquents to rate the consequences of rule breaking (cheating on an examination) behavior as important, probable, and severe.

In juveniles, Calicchia, et al. (1993) found that violent juveniles tended to be younger males whose families had a history of criminal behavior and extensive family discord. Moreover, the cognitive variables showed that violent youth showed differences in attention and memory, especially when they were processing violent stimuli. The following case illustration demonstrates the concrete thought processes of the violent youth.

The Case of Leon: His Need for Revenge

Leon was youth of borderline intellectual functioning. His mother had been an alcoholic and he suffered from Fetal Alcohol Syndrome. In addition, he had suffered severe environmental deprivation and abuse during his early childhood. His mother frequently abandoned him and was grossly neglectful of him. He was removed from his home and placed in emergency foster care. Two days later, he set fire to the house. The foster parents were both severely burned and their child was killed by smoke asphyxiation. Leon was placed in a specialized, secure residential treatment center.

He adapted well to the highly structured treatment program and seemed to enjoy the rules and order, which he had never before known. Each child at the program had his or her own footlocker to keep those items allowed in the program. To discourage theft, each locker had a small padlock. Some youth that had demonstrated sufficient responsibility were allowed to keep the key to the lock themselves, rather than having it stored in the staff office.

One of Leon's proudest moments was the day that he was given his footlocker key. Rather than carrying it on a string around his neck, as was the manner of the other youth, he managed to obtain a key clip from a staff member who had taken a particular liking to him. This key clip greatly resembled one worn by the staff and Leon took great pride in his clip. The treatment team interpreted his pride as, potentially, visible evidence, that he was beginning to identify in a positive manner with staff.

There was but one problem. Technically, it was against the rules of the facility for the youth to have such key clips. For some reason, never clearly understood, youth that held keys were required to either wear them around their necks or keep them on a ring in his or her pocket. Leon's team, however, chose to ignore this rule and make a special exception for Leon since it seemed so important to him.

One day, most of the regular staff was away for an in-service. A new staff member, on probation, saw Leon's key clip and knew that youth were not allowed to have such things. He took the clip and kept Leon's key in the staff office. As would be expected, Leon became extremely upset. He became agitated and combative to the degree that he required physical restraint.

The next day, the team returned and discovered, to their shock, what had happened. They called Leon into the team meeting to talk about what had happened. They asked Leon how he felt. He quickly and angrily replied that he wanted "to get back" at the staff member who had taken his key ring. He said that he wanted to "get him." The team, becoming concerned asked Leon just what he was planning to do. In a statement reflecting clear purpose and conviction, Leon stated that he planned to go find the new staff member. When he found him, Leon planned to extract his revenge by taking away the staff member's own keys.

There is, of course, more to violence than just thought processes. While anger and other emotions are not necessary for violence (for example in the case of a "contract" killer or "hit man," emotions often play an important role in violent behavior. Thus, we shall now turn to a discussion of the development of emotions and how this relates to the development of aggression.

Chapter 6

Affective Development

The development of our emotions follows in much the same manner as that of our thought. Many years ago, Bridges (1933) first observed that emotions gradually differentiate and become more complex, much as the same way that thought processes develop in the model of Piaget. More recently, developmental psychologists such as Kagen have suggested that emotions become gradually more complex after arising from certain basic temperamental states.

AFFECTIVE RESPONSES

Violent persons operate under a level of cognitive arousal higher than nonviolent individuals and may be seen as stimulation seekers. Arousal is the state of excitement or energy of the person. In a sense, it is the level of "drive" behind the psychological state of the youth. Arousal is a general phenomenon that is cued from specific stimuli. Some stimuli may be a result of environmental or exogenous circumstances and other stimuli may be internal or endogenous. As such, it is important, however to distinguish between the state of arousal that may be structurally or neurochemical based in origin and the aggressive act that is most often cognitively mediated and cued by triggers in the environment. In regards to affective expression, violent individuals tend to have a very narrow band of emotional expression, are concrete in their perceptions of their own emotions, and have difficulty in modulating affective expression. As noted, they are frequently seen as being unhappy or unwell (dysphoric). Aggressive individuals may also be dichotomized as habitually undercontrolled or overcontrolled in their expression of anger.

BIOLOGICAL FACTORS

Research in the past decade has resulted in intriguing evidence concerning the manner in which certain brain neurotransmitters may play a role in an individual's vulnerability or tendency to participate in aggressive behavior. An inverse relationship has been demonstrated between various measures of serotonin (5-HT) and aggressive behavior. Specifically, a reduced level of central serotonin system function and measures of irritability and aggressiveness. This has included studies that found lowered Cerebral Spinal Fluid concentrations of 5-hydroxyindoleacetic acid in aggressive populations, when compared to a normal sample. As well, mean platelet (^{3}H) serotonin uptake was significantly lowered in studies of aggressive individuals when compared to normal samples.

It has also been shown, as well, that noradrenergic system abnormality is evidenced in the aggressive clinical population. Growth hormone responses to the alpha-2 adregenic agonist clonidine are significantly greater in aggressive individuals and correlate positively with self-reports of irritability. As such, it appears that the more irritable a person is, the greater the sensitivity of the alpha-2 receptor and the greater sensitivity of the noradrenergic system to respond to novel or aversive stimuli.

Donovan (1997) has described ten cases of adolescents who evidenced chronic temper outbursts and mood lability. These youth were treated with divalproex sodium and showed clear improvement after five weeks and maintained it during follow-up while taking medication. It is suggested that this medication may be helpful to a subtype of youth who have explosive tempers and who also show mood swings. Because of their tempers and mood shifts, they often show chronic problems in both home and in school. Stabilizing their moods and tempers with divalproex sodium can allow for other forms of psychotherapy intervention such as cognitive and family therapies. Such youth have been termed by Donovan as suffering from an "explosive mood disorder."

In a study of under-controlled pre-adolescents, Weinberger and Gomes (1998) found that the morning moods of boys with disruptive behavior disorders did predict subsequent behavior, even when individual differences and previous day's behaviors were controlled.

This suggests that the mood changes of the boys may serve as a mediator between the intensity of the interpersonal conflict and problems in self-control of aggression. Additionally, it was found that youth who showed the highest denial of subjective distress were the ones who had the strongest links between mood and behavior. Taken together, these recent findings suggest that affective processes may play a substantial role in treatment of aggressive youth. This finding is potentially quite significant since much of the current treatment is based primarily upon cognitive and social factors. As will be seen in later chapters, the paradigm suggested in this work utilizes specific affective interventions such as creative therapies to address other "learning channels" of aggressive youth.

We shall, in the next chapter, pull these factors together and look at what we know specifically about aggressive and resistant youth in treatment settings. We shall, as well, explore risk factors, risk assessment, and dangerousness.

Chapter 7

Clinical Characteristics
of Violent Youth

The violent youth is most often a young male and is frequently seen by staff as evidencing greater disturbance than nonviolent youth on the staff's measures of emotional functioning. They show lowered empathy, insight, and are highly defensive, guarded, vigilant, and distrustful. When interviewed to ascertain their justification for their violent acts, they consistently report a concern over issues of fair play, and a review of instances of violence finds that denial of a privilege is the most frequent trigger for violent behavior in residential settings. Violent youth exhibit a marked sensitivity to being touched and require much "personal space." When interviewed, violent youth often express concern over their hostile urges and exhibit a higher level of cognitive arousal and dysphoria (suggesting the terminology of Donovan (1997) of "Explosive Mood Disorder."

Dynamically, these youth view destructiveness as part of the normal processes of life, having been given de facto permission to be violent by parental-role modeling. They have a negative self-concept and limited frustration tolerance, and this interaction often leads to a violent response to interpersonal conflicts. Violence is often a response to feelings of helplessness, and powerlessness and is sometimes a consequence of a struggle with depression and fear: they attack because they are afraid of being attacked. Violence can also be a solution to an impasse and a tension-release mechanism. Violence, especially in therapy and in committed relationships, can be a separative attempt. In other individuals, in contrast, violence can become an attempt, perhaps the only way, to make contact.

PSYCHOLOGICAL TESTING
AND PSYCHIATRIC DIAGNOSIS

There are no consistent psychological test findings that predict violence, especially in the case of adolescents. The research, as is often the case, focuses primarily on adults and may have only limited applicability to adolescents, particularly younger ones. In reference to adults, Serin and Amos (1995) found that the Hare Psychopathy Checklist—revised was a valid predictor of violent recidivism in an incarcerated sample. The Hare PCL-R has been consistently identified as an instrument that has promise for prediction of aggressive behaviors in adults. However, the Hare PCL-R has only limited research support for the use of the it with adolescents (Hare, 1995) This, of course, makes logical sense if the construct of psychopathy is understood in the context of developmental pathways. Characterlogical or Personality Traits do not arise overnight. Thus, an instrument such as the Hare would logically be potentially very useful at least for older adolescents and there appears to be research support for this argument.

Although often used in a correctional setting, the MMPI-A and its earlier version, the MMPI (interpreted without the K scale) has a mixed record of success in the prediction of aggressive behavior. When the traditional clinical scales are the only scales utilized, predictive validity of violence suffers greatly. The work of Megargee (1984) has resulted in a preliminary classification system of juvenile offenders using MMPI-A data.

It may well be that the problem is not with the system, but how that system is utilized. The MMPI has not had a robust history of accurate classification of an individual into diagnostic groups. However, the MMPI-2, when used for the purpose of clinical, behavioral, descriptions and inferences about a person (Graham, 1993) rather than "shotgun" clinical group differentiation application, has been found to be a useful component in the overall process of the prediction of aggressive behavior (Heilbrun, 1992). This is likely especially the case with the MMPI-A. MMPI-A interpretations do not utilize traditional code types given the lack of research support at present. This lends to a more differential approach in interpretation since the examiner must discern the relationship between profile elevations. Even more relevant to the study of aggression, however, are the MMPI-A content scales

(Williams et al., 1996). When taken with clinical profile elevations, content scales such as A-Ang, A-Cyn, and others can be quite helpful in the clinical description of the individual youth. (Ben-Porath and Davis, 1996).

With three highly significant exceptions, there is no relationship between any specific psychiatric diagnosis and violence. This is understandable, of course, because DSM IV categories are broad and encompass a wide variety of individuals within the classification schemes for various disorders. However, certain disorders do have a higher overall rate of violence when compared to others. But, the simple fact of a diagnosis is not, in and of itself, predictive of aggression in youth. It is known, in reference to specific diagnoses that reviews of violent youth consistently find evidence of a significantly higher rate of seizure disorders. Other research has yielded some findings of structural abnormalities, frequently in the limbic areas of the brain, as well as other nonspecific neurological abnormalities. Similar data also suggest serotonin imbalances as associated with violence.

Similar to that noted in the earlier cited work of Steadman (1998) in the McArthur Foundation research with adults, a coexisting diagnosis in violent youth of substance abuse is often reported. Recidivist assaultive youth have a higher rate of diagnosis of organic brain dysfunction, mood disorders, are male, tend to be overrepresented in minority groups and assault persons perceived as being weaker (Davis and Boster, 1987; Davis, 1991). Recent work by Circincione, Steadman, Robbins and Monahan (1992) suggested that a diagnosis of schizophrenia is becoming a risk factor in violence, where in earlier studies, this was not the case.

RISK FACTORS

The current research on risk assessment, such as Steadman (1998) as well as Heilbrun (1992) suggest that there is now a third generation of violence research. This concept suggests that one should consider first of all, risk factors. That is, what are the variables that one will use in the prediction of aggressive or violent behavior? Recent research has suggested that there are a number of characteristics about a person which, singularly or taken together, tend to increase the risk of violent behavior.

Breaking this down, one aspect that the correctional practitioner should consider is specifically, what type of harm is being predicted. As we have attempted to demonstrate in earlier chapters, violence is not a unitary phenomenon. There are many different kinds of violence. There is, of course, a clear difference between striking a person with one's fist in the heat of anger and stalking a victim for many months waiting for a clear shot with a sniper rifle. In another example, a person with a history of domestic violence is more likely to commit another act of domestic violence rather than other types of violence (of course persons with a history of domestic violence are at greater risk for all types of violence). Thus, the prediction of aggressive behavior needs to specify what specific type of violence is expected, or not expected.

Another area of consideration is that of the actual risk level. We all, for example, run a risk of being a victim of random shootings. However, this risk level is, of course, quite small. In fact, we are more likely to be killed by lightning than we are by random gunfire. But, if we are made the specific target of a threat of violence uttered by a person who has attacked us in the past, our risk level logically increases.

The Deadly Rorschach Cards

Some years back, as an intern, I was assigned the task of psychologically assessing a paranoid schizophrenic who had been hospitalized for many years. Not unexpectedly, he was rather distant and said very little during our clinical interview. To my surprise, he did agree to complete a battery of psychological tests. He wordlessly, but correctly copied all of the Bender Gestalt figures, a screening test for some types of brain damage. When shown the Rorschach Inkblot cards, as would be expected for a chronically mentally ill person, gave only minimal responses to the first three cards. However, when presented with card IV (all of those reading this with a psychoanalytic bent will now raise their eyebrows), he stared at it for a while. He then, keeping his eyes focused on the card, began to rise slowly from his chair. As he was getting up, he began to shake and said, "This card is telling me to kill you." I quickly suggested that we look at another card.

Monahan and Steadman (1992) suggest that risk factors be categorized into the following categories, *Static and Dynamic.* Static factors are those which are unchangeable through any intervention or form of intervention. Examples of such factors are age, gender, and aggression History. Dynamic factors are those personal or situational characteristics that might aggravate or mitigate the risk of aggression in the immediate case. Examples of these include substance abuse, Threat/Control Override Symptoms, anger, impulsivity, weapon access, unemployment, and social support. Thus, the variables outlined in previous portions of this chapter fall into either one or the other of these general categories.

Clinical Aggression Risk Variables

There are a number of risk variables which can be addressed in the assessment of risk and, as well, in the design of treatment interventions.

Psychopathy

Again, as identified previously, the clinical variable of psychopathy has been clearly associated with increased risk of violence. This, of course, makes logical sense; a chronically aggressive individual is, by definition, a person who lacks in empathy and respect for the rights of others. The Hare PCL-R, as noted above, is one of only two instruments (the other being the MMPI) which have demonstrated empirical support for use in assessment of the risk of violence in adults. This is likely, as stated by Hare (1991) because psychopaths demonstrate a personality structure and worldview that demeans the rights of others and promotes aggressive victimization of persons. Hare reports a number of well designed studies, including Hare and McPherson (1984) which found that 73 psychopaths defined by the PCL were significantly more likely than 154 other criminals to engage in physical violence and other criminal behavior. Wong (1984) found the same type of association. Harper and Hare (1991) suggested that, at least for posdiction of violent behavior in a criminal sample that the persons who scored high on both factor 1 and factor 2 of the PCL-R (using a multiple regression) were significantly more likely to engage in aggressive, violent behavior. As noted earlier, the Hare PCL-R shows promise for assessment of youth but has yet to receive enough research data to support its clinical use with adolescents. What can be drawn from this, of course, is that the clinical construct of psychopathy is a significant factor to be assessed in adolescents. In youth, a significant component of psychopathy development would be the combination of a significant (and early) conduct disorder as well as an Attachment Disorder.

Anger

While it is true that certain, rare types of violent individuals such as contract killers are generally nonemotional; anger appears to have a significant role in predisposition to violence as well as the actual violent behavior. It is for this reason that anger management programs are often a key component to aggression reduction treatment programs.

Impulsiveness

While certain types of violent behavior are instrumental and directed, such as the youth who carefully studies and stalks and intended victim, much of the violent behavior seen in an institutional setting is the result of poor impulse control. Often these individuals lack the ability to understand the consequences of their actions. Lacking in problem solving skills, they act impulsively, with little regard for or understanding of what will happen afterwards. Later, when apprehended or in facing the consequences of their actions in some other way, they may become overwhelmed with either remorse or self-pity (or both). At such times, they frequently become at risk for hurting themselves. Mentally ill youth that show some type of neurological impairment due to substance abuse, trauma or developmental factors are especially likely to be impulsive in their anger. Typically in an institutional setting, they run afoul of the rules and structures. If faced with a rigid staff member, the combination of the staff's unwillingness (or inability) to yield and the youth' poor problem solving, results in an impulsive angry action. Many of these youth are the types of person who, if able to be given a few minutes time out from the environmental stresses, are able to compose themselves and regain control.

It is also the case that a good percentage (perhaps larger than once realized) of mentally ill youth were once attention deficit disordered youth. Some adults still carry residual attention deficit disorders. Those that do not show the neurological signs still are hampered by their lack of positive experience in problem solving or in gratification delay.

Delusions

If there is one clinical sign of likelihood for aggression, it is the combination of paranoid thinking and antisociality. Mentally ill youth that have developed paranoid delusions often believe that they are being threatened and are often in great danger. They may, as well, experience command hallucinations that further reinforce their sense of danger.

Again drawing from the research on adults to illustrate this point, Link, Andrews, and Cullen (1992) compared mental patients and never treated community residents from a high crime area of New York City using a variety of official and self-report measures. Psychiatric patients were found to have higher rates on all measures of violent/illegal behavior. These behaviors could not be accounted for by sociodemographic and/or community context variables. A scale of psychotic symptoms (the false beliefs and perceptions scale from the Psychiatric Epidemiology Research Interview as well as thirteen items such as feeling possessed, feeling thoughts were not one's own and beliefs of mind control) was the only variable which accounted for the difference in violent behavior. Once again, while generalization from adults to adolescents is not supported by this data, clear clinical implications may be drawn.

Hallucinations

Resnick (1997) has implicated command hallucinations as an indication of increased risk of violence. When coupled with paranoid beliefs of thought control, behavioral control or persecution, command hallucinations can be a highly significant clinical indication of risk of violent behavior.

Threat/Control Override Symptoms

Threat/Control Override Symptoms is a concept which suggests that in certain individuals, the sense of perceived threat can more easily override psychological controls of violent behavior than in others. An illustration of this type of person would be an youth that has a lengthy history of paranoid thinking and an equally lengthy history of attacking others on the basis of this perceived threat. Such a person operates under a high degree of threat that easily overrides what are probably limited basic abilities to control his violent urges.

Social Support

Consistently, research (Monahan and Steadman, 1992) has linked isolation and lack of social support with violent behavior. Rice and Harris (1993) discuss a small group of youth who are severe management problems in a prison setting, have active psychotic symptoms and present with a number of management problems, including violence. They also appear depressed, lacking in social skills and are also frequently suicidal.

Demographic Factors

As noted earlier, violence is a behavior that is generally associated with a small group of people. In correctional settings, as well as in the community, a minority of individuals is responsible for the majority of violent behaviors. Toch (1982) classifies such persons as "disturbed-disruptive" It is suggested that, as is the case with disruptive persons in the community, that this small group of youth drains a disproportionate amount of resources in the correctional setting. Other demographic factors such as age, socio-economic status and gender appear to be equally relevant in the correctional population as they are in the community setting.

DANGEROUSNESS INDEX

Heilbrun and Heilbrun (1985) in the *British Journal of Clinical Psychiatry* compared correlations between simple psychopathy and IQ and between psychopathy and withdrawal typologies among 225 male prisoners (mean age 26.8 years) who had been seen for parole evaluation by psychologists as part of a mandatory parole review by a pardons and parole board. It was hypothesized that dangerousness would be correlated with low IQ and social withdrawal tendencies. Results from measures of psychopathy, intelligence, social withdrawal in combination with records of prior criminal violence and disciplinary records of prison misbehavior (dangerousness) confirmed the dangerousness of psychopathic subjects with low IQ and/ or social withdrawal tendencies in their prison behavior and low IQ psychopaths on parole. A successful attempt was made to develop a more homogeneous typology for dangerous psychopaths by increasing the number of defining attributes. Those subjects who shared these attributes obtained the highest prison and parole dangerousness scores in the prisoner sample: Psychopathy, low IQ, social withdrawal, and history of prior violent crime.

These studies suggest that the highest risk is a combination of Low IQ and High Antisociality. Those on index were more likely to have committed a violent crime than nonviolent (property). Men committing more severe forms of criminal violence were higher on the index than those committing less serious violence. Individuals sentenced to death were higher on index than those receiving life sentences. Those displaying greater brutality in sexual offenses were higher on this index than those showing less brutality.

A final area of discussion of youth characteristics in the treatment of violence deserves special focus: homicidal adolescents. We shall now turn our discussion to this specialized (and growing) group of youth.

Chapter 8

The Homicidal Adolescent: Hearts Darkened Before Time

Adolescence was once a time of promise and light. Today, in our society, children and youth are being killed or are killing at an ever-increasing pace. According to the United States Department of Justice, nearly ten people each day are murdered by juveniles. Violence by youth in our society continues to increase at a frightening pace. Homicides in the United States by young men are four to seventy-three times higher than in other nations (Ewing, 1990). American males between fifteen and twenty-four years old are murdered at a rate of 21.9 per 100,000 (Ewing, 1990). Homicide is the leading cause of death of African-American males and females under the age of twenty-five. A young African-American male is eleven times more likely to die by homicide than a non-African-American male. Every year, on average, more than 1,500 American youngsters under the age of eighteen take the life of another person and are arrested for murder or manslaughter. This statistic does not take into account those youth that intended to kill but were either stopped or were unsuccessful in the attempt to murder (Ewing, 1990).

In the 1970s there were no homicides attributed to gangs. In 1980, there were 351 gang-related homicides. Between 1985 and 1989, there were over 1,500 gang-related homicides. There are over 200 million firearms owned by private citizens in the United States. It is estimated that students carry 270,000 handguns into school each day. The percentage of homicides committed by youth continues to increase. For the first time, in 1988, the percentage increased beyond 10 percent and has continued to climb. It is predicted that the 1990s will show the highest annual rates of juvenile homicides in American history and current trends support this prediction (Ewing, 1990).

Despite these trends, the proportion of youth that kill remains small. Currently, fewer than five juveniles out of every 100,000 are arrested for homicide. The majority of these youth are ages fifteen or over. The number of below the age of fifteen who murder is small and those under ten are but a handful (Ewing, 1990). Although youth rarely kill, they do commit other crimes. Nearly one-third of all property crimes are committed by juveniles and youth under the age of eighteen consistently account for 17 to 20 percent of all crimes (Ewing, 1990).

Juveniles have become, as well, increasingly vulnerable to victimization, primarily by other juveniles. An estimated 2,660 juveniles were murdered in 1994, a rate of seven youth killed per day. Four times as many juveniles were killed with a gun in 1994 than in 1984. One in five murdered juveniles were killed by another juvenile and more than half of the victims were between fifteen and seventeen. Thus, in the past twenty years, the responsibility of juveniles for the growth in violent crimes has substantially increased. The rate of juveniles murdered in 1994 was nearly twice that of those murdered in 1994.

RESEARCH REVIEW OF CHARACTERISTICS
OF JUVENILE MURDERS

The vast majority of youth arrested for homicide are males. Those few girls who kill tend to kill family members (Ewing, 1990). While ethnic and race variables are important considerations, it is socioeconomic status that facilitates the higher rates of violence among minority ethnic groups. Roughly one-sixth of all Americans under the age of eighteen are African American, in recent years, approximately one half of the youth arrested for homicide are African American. In 1988, over 57 percent of the juveniles arrested for homicide were African American.

Approximately 8 percent of the population in the United States are Hispanic and Hispanic youth account for almost one-quarter of the juvenile arrests for homicide crimes. (Ewing, 1990). It is widely acknowledged that ethnic groups tend to commit violent crimes primarily within their own groups and it is further acknowledged that minority youth are more likely to be arrested and sent to correctional rather than treatment facilities.

Since adolescent homicide, for the time being, remains fairly rare, those youth arrested tend to be seen by mental health professionals. Most youth are assigned a diagnosis but the classification is rarely that of a psychosis. Rather, either conduct disorder or emerging personality disorders tend to be given as diagnoses. Most youth arrested for homicide tend to have average to above average IQs (Ewing, 1990).

A considerable body of research, generally using single cases or very small samples, found over representations of neurological impairments in homicidal adolescents. Abnormalities such as epilepsy, EEG abnormalities, limbic and reticular activating system disorders, learning disabilities and neonatal deficits are often seen (Busch et al., 1990).

Freud (1939), in the *Standard Edition* (Vol. 21) postulated those child murderers, who had death wishes toward parents had inconsistent parenting, witnessed violence, experienced physical abuse and suffered rejection. Bender (1959), in her clinical descriptions presented five circumstances: (1) severe family rivalry, (2) inability of a parent or guardian to curb aggressiveness, (3) organic inferiority and deprivation, (4) insurmountable educational difficulties, and (5) severe familial aggressiveness.

Lewis, (1985) found four symptoms associated with adolescent murders: violent fathers, seizures, suicidal tendencies, and psychiatrically hospitalized mothers. Cornell, Benedek, and Benedek (1987) reviewed seventy-two cases in Michigan in pretrial evaluations over a nine-year period. They were compared with a control group of thirty-five youth charged with nonviolent larceny offenses. Few of the homicide group had a history of mental health treatment prior to the offense and only five were assessed as psychotic at the time of the offense.

A significant exception to this is the Lewis (1988) study of fourteen youth condemned to die and awaiting execution on a death row. In this group, one was mentally retarded, and only two had IQ's in the normal range. Also, in this group, each subject had symptoms consistent with neurological impairment (a finding generally replicated in diagnostic evaluations of violent individuals). Eight of the youth had experienced head injuries severe enough to warrant hospitalization and/or indentation of the cranium and nine had serious documented neurological abnormalities which included focal brain injury, abnormal head circumference, abnormal reflexes, seizure disorders, and abnormal EEGs.

Cornel, Miller, and Benedek, (1988) investigated MMPI profiles of thirty-six adolescent murderers and a control group of eighteen adolescents charged with larceny. The subjects were from twelve to nineteen years old. Homicide cases were subgrouped into those who committed homicide secondary to another crime such as robbery or rape and those who acted within the context of interpersonal conflict with the victim. Overall, it was found that adolescents charged with homicide, as a group did not differ significantly from control group adolescents. Although this may seem surprising, and may reflect trends in court referrals for evaluations, it does suggest that seriousness of the crime does *not* correspond to the severity of psychopathology, as assessed by the MMPI. While there were no significant differences between the homicide and larceny groups, crime and conflict subgroups were significantly different on scales F, Hs (1), Hy (3), and Sc (8) with the crime group scoring in the more deviant direction. As such, crime group youth appeared to youth appear to be experiencing significantly higher feelings of distress and alienation together with limited insight and likely somatization defenses. The mean MMPI profile of the homicide/crime group was an 8-6-4 profile and was similar to adolescents who exhibit impulsive behavior and who have violent tempers. Such youth tend to come from markedly dysfunctional families, are unsuccessful in school and have highly conflictual interpersonal relationships. The homicide/conflict groups mean profile (4-6-8) was subclinical. Psychiatric diagnoses of each of the groups were quite diverse. Overall, the finding of the research was that while no consistent MMPI pattern of homicidal youth was obtained, youth who commit homicide in the context of a crime presented a much more elevated MMPI than those who killed in an interpersonal situation. Over all, the findings suggest a clear need for a more differentiated approach to the study of adolescent homicides.

Busch et al. (1990) studied 1956 adolescents ages ten through seventeen referred by courts for examinations. Of these, seventy-one who were convicted of homicide were matched with seventy-one nonviolent youth. On the basis of stepwise discriminant analysis, it was found that four characteristics differentiated the two groups: criminally violent family members, gang membership, severe educational difficulties, and alcohol abuse.

In one of the few studies addressing the interpersonal context of adolescent homicide, Duncan and Duncan (1971) presented five cases in which a homicidal adolescent's abrupt loss of control was related to a change in his interpersonal relationship with the victim and a sequence of events progressively more unbearable and less amenable to control. Potential of violence within the family was characterized by criteria such as intensity of verbal expression of destructive impulses, availability of weapons and provocativeness of the intended victim. A history of parental brutality was also found to be an important consideration.

Ewing (1990) posits that homicidal behavior is learned and is a function of person and circumstance. In a review of the literature, he indicates that nearly all cases reported involve youth that have been significantly influenced by one of the following factors: child abuse, poverty, substance abuse, and access to guns.

In a study of twenty-five homicidal youths, Myers (1998) found that 96 percent of them evidenced DSM-III-R pathology and over half had experienced suicidal ideation but only 17 percent had actually received mental health services. Family and school dysfunction was present in most of the youth. Typically, the youth had histories of abuse, prior violence and arrests, and promiscuous sexual behavior.

TYPOLOGIES

Given the dearth of data on adolescent homicides, few research-based topologies exist. The most promising is that of Myers (1998) which suggests using the FBI Crime Classification Manual. It was noted that in this sample of twenty-five youth, the motives were equally divided between crime-based and conflict-based causes. A weapon was used in 96 percent of the cases. The crime classification system was able to differentiate between the classification groups in the areas of victim age, physical abuse, IQ, and victim relationship. It was also noted that those youth involved in sexual homicide were likely to have engaged in overkill, used a knife and had been armed prior to the murder. Ten profile characteristics were identified in 70 percent of the sample: family dysfunction, previous violent acts towards others, disruptive behavior disorders, failure of at least one school grade, family member emotional abuse, family violence, prior arrests, learning disabilities, weapon of choice, and psychotic symptoms.

Cornel, Benedek, and Benedek, (1987) investigated a typology of three major distinctions of juvenile homicides (psychotic, conflict, and criminal). Case records from 1977 through 1985 of seventy adolescents ages twelve through eighteen and thirty-five adolescents (ages fifteen through eighteen) were compared. Information on fifty-two background variables clustered into eight composite categories (family dysfunction, school adjustment, childhood problems, violence history, delinquent behavior, substance abuse, psychiatric problems, and stressful life events prior to the offense) were coded. Youth charged with larceny scored higher on composite measures of school adjustment, childhood symptoms, criminal history, and psychiatric history. There were, as well, significant differences between the subtypes of homicide. This chapter will present clinical case illustrations of the subtypes identified by Benedek.

THE PSYCHOTIC ADOLESCENT MURDERER

Case Study: Kenneth

Kenneth is a fifteen-year-old Caucasian male who had been living with his mother until his arrest for the murder of his sixteen-year-old cousin. He was born after a normal pregnancy and birth to a sixteen-year-old mother. His mother later completed two years of college and entered a successful career in public service. He was raised with his cousin, almost as siblings. He was physically healthy but was temperamentally described as a "difficult child." In contrast, his cousin was described as a pleasant, articulate, and bright girl. Kenneth slept poorly and cried frequently at night. Gross motor development was normal but he was seen at a pediatric center for "slow" speech beginning at age two and one half. At age three, he was treated with Ritalin for hyperactivity. He was described as evidencing numerous conduct problems and was described as "unsociable." At age five, he entered kindergarten where he was seen as a responsible child who completed his work and was not a behavioral problem.

When he was in the eighth grade, he and his mother moved to their present home that was in a new school district. Shortly after the move, he began to isolate himself from peers. He attended school, but had no friends or social interests. He would return home to watch television, listen to rap music, or play with army figures. As he progressed through school, he continued to be more isolated. His grandmother began to worry about his unusual behavior and shortly after that, he began to project anger toward her, deliberately breaking her belongings, stealing things, and creating a mess in her home. He became sullen, rude toward her, and frequently would attempt to ignore her.

In the summer before the homicide, he spent most of his time watching television. He became extremely territorial. At home, he became extremely territorial. The family room and television became his room and no one was welcomed into his bedroom. He did not allow anyone to change channels on the television or direct any actions in "his world." Over time, the family accommodated to him and did not challenge this behavior.

The day before the murder, the cousin moved into Kenneth's house so that she could attend a different high school. She hoped to become a cheerleader and become involved in student council. This move was not discussed with Kenneth and was a surprise to him. The cousin, as well, put her things in Kelvin's room because she did not yet have a place for them. On the day of the murder, it is reported that she turned on "his TV," changed channels without his permission, picked up the portable telephone without his permission and began to call friends. She, as well, spoke about the activities she planned to join in school, made derogatory remarks about his grades and, lastly, laid on his blanket in the family room.

Official police reports indicate that the victim was talking on the telephone with her boyfriend for about one hour. During that hour, she had several brief conversations with Kenneth. The boyfriend heard her drop the telephone, scream "Call my house!" and then heard several gunshots. The boyfriend called the mother and told her what happened. She went home and found her sister suffering from several gunshot wounds. Kenneth and her handgun, a .38 revolver, were missing.

In a forensic interview, Kenneth related that he was extremely upset that his cousin was moving in with him and would attend the same school. He recalled that she had brought a "bag of her stuff to my room." She then turned on the TV and started talking to her boyfriend. He stated that he felt that she was going to "take over." He felt scared and nervous and that "my presence wasn't there." He then remembers seeing her pick up his grade card and laughing at it. He felt more nervous and scared. He then went and got the gun. He stated that he felt like he was someone else at the time and that the gun was not real.

In the forensic psychological evaluation, he was found to evidence a severe degree of psychopathology on the Rorschach. He was described as presenting a productive and vivid protocol. Both form and content were distorted, convoluntional, and reflective of delusional thought. Content indicated a perception of interpersonal relationships as threatening and hostile. Confabulation and distortion marked the responses. Emotional control was seen as quite poor and developmentally delayed. He was seen has being extremely emotionally detached. The summary impression of the protocol was a similarity to schizophrenic records, that he had little emotional control in reference to thoughts and feelings with distorted and delusional thinking. The TAT record was striking in its brevity. Of note was that even his limited responses were nearly completely unrelated to the events portrayed on the cards. Analysis of the offense found that the shooting was a result of his delusional fear of his cousin's entering into his "domain." Although she had no idea of the threat she posed, her behavior pushed him far past his limited defense mechanisms. The actions of changing his television channels, going into his room, commenting on his grades and using the telephone are seemingly "normal and expected" behaviors. Because of his thought disorder and delusional system, he became threatened, lost track of the reality of the situation, depersonalized and saw no other way out of the situation but to remove the threat by killing her.

Upon admission to a closed residential treatment center, he was initially seen as withdrawn, noncommunicative, and hostile. He was placed on an anti-psychotic medication and seen in individual and family therapy. A behavioral program limiting his isolation was implemented. After eighteen months, he was transferred to an open residential setting from which he was eventually placed in a treatment foster home.

THE CRIMINAL ADOLESCENT MURDERER

Case Study: Donald

Donald, a sixteen-year-old, white male, was evaluated in a question of waiver or bindover to the adult system. He was charged with one count of aggravated murder, aggravated robbery, aggravated burglary, and theft. He and another youth broke out of a state juvenile correctional facility and traveled to a small town, which was the home of the other youth. They went to the house of an elderly man whom had testified against the other youth, attacked and beat him, robbed his house, and kidnapped the victim by placing him in the trunk of his car. They then drove to a bridge and threw the victim off of a bridge. Although he was apparently alive when thrown from the bridge, he died upon impact.

At the time of forensic evaluation, Donald was in the lock up area of the correctional facility, having attacked and threatened to kill a staff member.

Records indicated that he was the second of four children from an extremely problematic childhood characterized by substance abuse, physical abuse, neglect, and instability. All of the children were in the care of various agencies and the family was described as highly resistant to treatment. He was diagnosed as hyperactive in the first grade and became involved in the juvenile justice system at age eight. His first out of home placement took place at age eleven. He was placed in juvenile correctional facilities at age twelve following an attempt to stab another youth. At age fourteen, he attempted to strangle a youth with a belt. His juvenile court record subsequently contained charges of attacks upon others, holding a knife to a child's throat, arson, and carrying a concealed weapon. Assaultive behavior, self-mutilation, escape, and suicidal threats characterized his institutional placement. Clinically, he was seen as Attention Deficit Hyperactive Disorder, and a severe Conduct Disorder. No evidence of psychosis was ever reported. Intellectually, he consistently presented within the borderline range of general intelligence.

In forensic evaluation, he was found to report an extensive history of physical abuse victimization but denied any sexual abuse. He reported as, well, an extensive history of substance abuse beginning at age nine. He described his temper control problems as "I just flip, any little thing can make me mad. I just strike out." He was able to relate the details of the alleged offense, had a clear working knowledge of the justice system, and expressed an understanding of the attorney youth relationship. On the WAIS-R, he was found to function within the borderline range of general intelligence with no significant advantage in verbal or performance skills. He was found to have strengths in social awareness and basic visual motor reproduction skills. Difficulties were seen in tasks requiring abstractions of either a verbal or visual motor nature and he had particular difficulty in tasks that required judgment. There was an indication of a learning disorder related to a limited attention span and visual perceptual processing difficulties. The Bender Gestalt found errors of rotation, angulation and distortion, and yielded a level of visual perceptual functioning below that expected for his age. Records of a similar nature are associated with learning disabilities. An MMPI was administered using a tape-recorded protocol and was found to be invalid. The Rorschach was not found to be indicative of psychosis but did suggest impulsivity, poor judgment, poor emotional control, and a view of interpersonal relationships as hostile and conflictual. He expressed no substantial regret for his actions, believing that the victim deserved his fate as he had turned in the other youth. He, as well, indicated that he preferred to be placed in the adult system because he wanted to go to prison. He did state that he was aware that if he was placed in the juvenile system, he would be out sooner and stated that, if returned to the community, he would "get busted again." He was assessed as not being amenable to further treatment in the juvenile justice system and was bound over to the adult court. He entered a plea of guilty to murder and received a sentence of twenty years to life with a possibility of parole within seven years.

INTERPERSONAL CONFLICT

Case Study: Bill

Bill was a twelve-year-old, white male, who shot another student in the cafeteria of his middle school. The youth was shot in the head with a revolver. Bill's father is sixty-two years old, an alcoholic, and on disability due to back injuries. He was married twice, and has a mentally retarded daughter. The mother is twenty years younger, and had been married three times before; the first of which was at age fifteen. There are two older siblings. The family moved frequently due to economic difficulties. The parents reported that the family did "everything together" and the youth were not allowed to spend time away from the house for long periods and were not allowed to go overnight to friends' houses. Bill's pregnancy, delivery, development, and current health were reported to be normal. Due to the frequent moving of the family, Bill had difficulty adjusting academically and socially to school. His grades tended to vacillate but he was generally well-liked by teachers and peers. However two months before the offense, his demeanor changed and his teachers saw him as having an "attitude problem." In reference to the shooting, the victim was a boy whom Bill described as having been "bullying" him. The night before, Bill saw the gun lying on the coffee table of his parent's house and took it and twelve bullets with him to school. At school, a friend asked him to hold some marijuana for him and Bill agreed. He met that boy sitting with the victim at the lunchroom. He stated that "I said to him, 'Hey Jim, he turned around, looked at me and I shot him. Everything was all quiet. I pointed the gun up in the air and shot it again. I went outside and shot it again into the ground. One of my teachers came up, I threw the gun away and said to him, 'I f....d up.'" In subsequent interviews, he reported no memory of shooting the victim. He later claimed that he did it so "No other kids would bother me."

In psychological testing, he was found to have a WISC-R verbal score of 105, a performance score of 98 and a full-scale score of 101. No significant subtest scatter was found. Projective personality testing found strong feelings of inferiority, inadequacy, and denial. He was seen as emotionally immature. No overt symptoms of psychosis were found. An over emphasis upon strength and power was found, however. He was seen as quite egocentric with some confusion of psychosexual and aggressive urges. Lastly, it was found that his conceptualization of intimacy more reflected the self-directed expression of his own immature needs.

The MMPI-A revealed multiple serious behavioral problems including school maladjustment, family discord, and authority conflicts. He was seen as moody, resentful, and attention seeking. He was described as impulsive, rebellious, and with poor judgment. Content scales suggested a likelihood for risk taking behaviors, immediate gratification, and numerous and serious behavioral problems. Self-reports of stealing, shoplifting, lying, and drug abuse were found. Supplemental scales suggested a strong probability for substance abuse.

This youth adapted well to a structured day treatment programming and received considerable in home wrap around services. Services included intensive family therapy as well as individual therapy addressing anger management and thinking errors. He has maintained in the community nonviolently for two years since the incident.

What can be done for youth and younger adults such as those described above? As stated by Myers (1998) little has been done, but much should be. Simple criminal sanctions and reduced rehabilitative efforts are, to use the eloquent term of Myers, "a short-sighted gambit." The following chapters will outline treatment approaches that have been successfully utilized in community based as well as residential and institutional settings. Chapter 9 will discuss general principals of treatment and also address issues surrounding discharge of the violent youth back into the community. Because many of the aggressive youth seen in treatment settings are court referred or involuntary, Chapter 10 will focus upon counseling approaches with resistant and unwilling youth.

Chapter 9

General Principles in the Treatment of the Violent Youth

As the nature of the violent youth is complex and interactive, interventions with violent youth cannot afford the illusionary parsimony of single approaches. Accordingly, a multidomain model of intervention (see Table 9.1) is required. Further, to treat the individual and ignore the dysfunctional environment of that person will only doom the intervention to failure even before it is begun. Violence is generally a lifelong difficulty, often resulting from perceived threat on the part of individuals who need to learn consistency in their lives. Accordingly, modification of violent behavior is not a rapid process, and involves commitment on the part of the clinician and the youth. Fortunately, violent individuals generally have times when they are open to such changes, and the clinician must be ready and available to respond. Further, counselors must be consistent in their interactions with youth. Violent youth are highly vigilant for perceived transgressions against them, and the clinician must strive to be open, fair, and willing to respond without defensiveness to the challenges of the violent youth.

The relationship formed with the aggressive youth is crucial. Violent individuals are often lonely, isolated, and dysphoric (factors that make them good candidates for intervention). The clinician must accept the individual while rejecting the violent behavior. The violent youth must understand the difference and will be hyperalert for any interpersonal rejection. The clinician must be ready for antisocial behavior on the part of the youth. The youth is likely to be initially untruthful and unreliable. The clinician must continue to accept the person, and as self-esteem and frustration tolerance of the youth increase, the aggressive behavior will likely decrease.

TABLE 9.1. Developmental Treatment Approaches Using Cognitive-Behavioral-Expressive Therapy

AGE	COGNITIVE	AFFECTIVE	BEHAVIORAL	SOCIAL
0-2	Awareness Early stimulation	Differentiation and organization of emotions	Basic motor skills exercises	Attachment Basic needs provision
2-5	Language development interventions Concrete problem solving tasks Acquisition of basic rules	Learning of appropriate means of emotional expression	Motor reproduction of behavior Gross locomotion skills	Initial social play Sibling/peer relationships Group interaction skills
5-12	Logical problem solving skill development Acquisition of perceptual flexibility Elementary and middle schools skills and remediation	Creative therapies Development of impulse control skills Development of affective modulation skills	Cognitive mediated behavior skills Fine motor skills Pre-vocational skills	Social recognition of actions Group cooperation and teamwork skills Positive reinforcement programs
12-Adult	Cognitive structuring and restructuring therapies Problem solving therapies Abstract moral reasoning	Anger management Stress Inoculation Autogenics Progressive relaxation Expressive therapies	Vocational skill development Assertiveness training Independent living skills	Organized group interactions Point/level systems Social role modeling

COGNITIVE INTERVENTIONS

The violent youth is likely to have a very narrow band of imaginative thought and is likely to habitually appraise situations in an aggressive manner and ruminate upon violent fantasies or self-perceptions. Accordingly, cognitive therapy should, with due consideration given to the fragile self-esteem of the violent youth, focus upon alternative appraisal mechanisms. In individual therapy, the use of a logbook of perceptions can help in recording thoughts and reinforcing nonviolent appraisals (the way the youth views the environment). In the group setting, art therapy techniques such as cartoons without captions can be quite useful to the same end. Youth should be given a nonviolent framework to counter learned perceptions. A lifeline drawn out using the Erikson stages of development can help youth make sense of what is perceived as generally chaotic early life experiences.

The clinician must be able to discuss the violent thoughts and fantasies of the youth. This will give control to the thoughts that should be allowed to be expressed and not challenged when they are stated in a safe, nonthreatening environment. The lack of expression of anger is often an indication that therapy is not progressing. However, expression of violent fantasies must be done with caution with psychotic and borderline youth. If it is seen that expression increases the strength of the thought, the clinician should change approaches and intervene by setting limits and providing increased structure if needed. With such youth, considerable caution is required. If, in the expression of such violent thoughts, a particular individual or circumstance is identified, and the youth has a realistic plan to harm a specific person, then consideration must be given to the therapist's duty to warn the intended victim.

The change of appraisals will require flexibility on the part of the clinician, as well. Because the violent youth is likely to have limited verbal skills and imaginative resources, the use of primarily verbally oriented interventions will be difficult. The use of art and other creative therapies, accordingly, can be quite valuable to help the youth develop and test out alternative appraisals and problem-solving approaches in a much safer setting than in vivo or even role-playing or group situations. As an illustration, violent youth can draw out possible consequences of aggressive behavior by the technique of sequential drawings. This approach consists of both describing and drawing a sequence of imagined behaviors and allows the clinician and youth to explore alternative views and fantasize alternative coping strategies. This technique allows the youth to produce a documented exploration of key issues in therapy and the potential consequences of various actions. Such drawings facilitate and support the therapeutic alliance by allowing engagement within a safe, structured environment.

Directed drawings in which the therapist instructs the youth to draw particular events or concepts also allow the youth to solve problems in a setting that allows for increase in mastery and efficacy via sequentially increasing nonviolent approaches. In this approach, it is possible for the youth to safely role-play various responses as well as allowing a means to re-experience trauma but with a directed, positive outcome. By participating in the process, the therapist becomes more of an equal partner and this alliance can assist in reducing threats the youth might feel in relationships with others. To be effective, either technique requires at least six frames of drawings but should not exceed ten. In drawing out the child, the therapist should "shadow" the child, staying within any metaphors the child might produce while drawing and, ultimately, allowing the youth to direct the drawing process. The child, lastly, can leave the nonfunctional approach behind in the therapy room, even to the symbolic extent of crumpling up the paper as way of demonstrating closure.

Finally, youth should never be relieved of their responsibility for their behavior. To allow them not to be responsible both gives license and psychologically increases their sense of helplessness and hopelessness.

AFFECTIVE INTERVENTIONS

As violent youth have difficulty with arousal (the state of excitement or energy of the person), the use of stress management techniques can be quite helpful. The use of anger management techniques, progressive relaxation techniques such as autogenics, together with somatic interventions can be helpful in reducing arousal. The clinician, as well, should not assume that the youth is able to identify emotional responses correctly this mislabeling will serve to potentially increase arousal. It has been noted that aggressive individuals tend to have overinclusive, concrete labels for emotions, generally identifying base-line states as being "happy-mad-sad-quiet" with limited awareness of gradients in between or discrimination of subtle states. Using colors and music can help the youth to identify varying emotional states, thus increasing a sense of mastery over the affective state. Because violent persons are usually concrete and overinclusive, it is often the case that proprioceptive cues (their own inner signals such as muscle tightening, increased heart rate, etc.) of arousal go unnoticed. The youth remains unaware of the psychophysiological concomitant of anger and simply "explodes." Accordingly, the use of art, music and movement thera-pies to identify and enhance proprioceptive awareness can lead to greater control and adaptive responses. Techniques of proprioceptive awareness can be linked into a structured autogenics progressive relax-ation procedure that can be initiated upon arousal.

BEHAVIORAL COPING SKILLS

Counselors should teach skills to youth that are likely lacking in basic social skills. A life-skill, positive adaptive-behavior model using empathy training an empathy-based assertiveness training is especially useful. Youth should leave each interchange with the clinician with some positive life-skill either a new one or one reinforced by the clinician. Each skill must be taught in a positive, nonjudgmental man-ner. Skills to be taught include those of conflict resolution, negotiation, compromise, gratification delay, and social interactions. These tech-niques are often begun individually and then expanded to group set-tings. Using films, role models, and other alternative media draws heavily upon the power of social learning, the means by which many of the aggressive behaviors were initially learned. Youth can also be taught to avoid situations where violence may take place.

ENVIRONMENTAL INTERVENTIONS

A key factor, then in the understanding of treatment approaches for violent persons is to recall that a substantial portion of chronically aggressive youth are either psychopaths or have strong psychopathic features. Thus, the traditional mental health interventions which do not address thinking error concepts tend to have very limited utility in the treatment of the violent youth. Successful programs must address not only anger management aspects (as noted below) but must also address errors of thinking (Samenow, 1995; Rice, 1996).

PITFALLS AND CLINICAL PROVOCATION OF VIOLENCE

Counselors should not ignore dangerousness. Revelation by youth of dangerous plans is often a cry for help, but one that engenders responses of counter-transference and psychological defensiveness on the part of the clinician. It is not uncommon for therapists to be anxious about the violence potential of their youth and to react to it by consciously or unconsciously denying the real potential for violence. At the same time, counselors should try to avoid overreacting. When at all possible, they should not place themselves in an adversarial role. When this happens, the clinician must clearly explain the basis for their actions and be ready to discuss it with the youth at some later date.

In reviews of assaults upon counselors, the victimized therapists frequently reported that it was likely that some action or statement by the clinician provoked the assault, and most felt that they could have anticipated the assault. Among the reasons given for the assaults were refusing to meet the youth's request, forcing youth to take medication, setting too many limits, not setting enough limits, transference reactions, homosexual panic by the youth in response to transference, and material being dealt with in therapy. Many counselors felt that they were too insistent in forcing a youth to confront upsetting materials. Some therapists reported that they did not like the youth that assaulted them and that this interpersonal dislike may have translated into interpersonal distance and an omnipotent facade that might trigger an assault. Other therapists indicated that they might have been too permissive and given the message that violence would be tolerated. In reference to milieu staff members' characteristics that increase violence, it has been shown that aggressive behavior is triggered by staff who are overstructured, authoritarian, and inflexible and who are inconsistent in behaviors and consequences. Fearful staff members produce fearful youth and, accordingly increase the likelihood of violence (Pinta and Davis, 1987).

THE DISCHARGE OF THE VIOLENT YOUTH

It is axiomatic that the discharge of the mentally disordered violent youth into the community requires considerable planning and active case management. These youth are often lacking in even the most basic social supports in the community. They tend to have alienated or have lost contact with family or friends. Faced with psychosocial stresses such as homelessness, lack of employment and isolation, they become quickly vulnerable to aggression disinhibiting agents such as alcohol and substance abuse. As is the case with the nonviolent mentally ill youth, predischarge planning and active case-management services are essential for the aggressive mentally ill youth (Axelrods and Wetzler, 1989).

Chapter 10

The Clinical Experience
of the Unwilling Youth

Frequently, in community and institutional correctional settings, mental health counselors encounter youth that are unwilling or resistant to enter into the counseling process. This unwillingness can show itself either overtly or covertly. The youth may overtly resist by refusing to attend sessions, being disruptive during the session or actively resisting any suggestions or interventions of the clinician. Covert resistance can be seen in passive aggressive behavior as well as attempts to manipulate or "con" the clinician. Counselors who are not experienced in correctional populations are often overwhelmed by the challenge of such youth. They may too easily give up on them as being untreatable, when it is frequently not the youth that is the problem but the expectations and methods of interventions of the counselor. This chapter will focus upon understanding and intervening with youth that are resistive to becoming involved in treatment.

An important initial consideration in the psychological treatment of violent youth is the frequently seen difference in how such youth are referred for mental health care. Often, violent and aggressive do not refer themselves voluntarily for treatment. Instead, they often come to services as a result of some type of requirement such as a court order, or to avoid an undesirable consequence such as incarceration or loss of privilege. The youth do not often see the problem as their problem. Rather, they experience the problem as belonging to others. In fact, the

---

The author is indebted to the creative and insightful work of Stanley L. Prods, one of the true leaders in the field of psychological interventions with a criminal justice population. The following two chapters reflect this debt and are dedicated to Dr. Brodsky.

primary problem that they may see is that they have been referred for counseling! As a result, these youth are often experienced by their counselors as being resistant, uncooperative or unwilling. Often, in their frustration, counselors grow quite pessimistic about the ability of these unwilling youth to make any positive clinical change. This frustration can result in the counselor using labels such as "hopeless," "unmotivated," or worst of all, "manipulative."

When first confronted with this type of youth, counselors in correctional setting can feel overwhelmed and ineffective. This is often do to an inherent role conflict that results from the training and expectations of mental health counselors. Traditional clinical training is based upon voluntary, nonresistive, verbal youth. However, in the correctional setting, counselors often encounter unwilling and resistant youth, for which they are unprepared. This lack of preparation results in misunderstandings, frustration and feelings of inadequacy on the part of the counselor (Davis and Brodsky, 1992).

THE FOUR TYPES OF MENTAL HEALTH PROBLEMS

Counselors who provide services to the unwilling youth need to remember that voluntary and involuntary youth approach the clinical experience with very different perceptions of problems. There are four types of problems:

Problems defined by the youth	Problems defined by the counselor
Problems defined by both the youth and the counselor	Problems not seen by the youth or the counselor

Problems Which the Clinician Defines

Especially in the case of the involuntary, referred youth, the problem that defines the need for counseling is often not seen by the youth. Instead, the youth/youth does something that violates the rules or norms of the facility and is, as a result, is sent to the mental health clinician. Thus, as and illustration, the counselor may be sitting quietly in his or her office, minding one's own business, when one of the staff gives a call, "Doc, are you busy? Youth So and So just shot off his mouth again and threw a coffee cup. I don't want to charge him, would you talk to him?" You agree. Youth So and So shows up in your office and plops down in a chair, obviously not thrilled to be spending time with you.

In a case such as this, the youth/youth doesn't really "own the problem." In fact, he or she may see nothing wrong with the behavior. Rather, the behavior is upsetting or disconcerting in some manner to those who either live with or must regulate the youth. This, of course, is quite typical in an youth counseling setting. Many times, the only problem the youth-counseling youth may actually see is that he or she has been forced to go into counseling.

Problems Which the Youth Defines

Beyond simply seeing the primary problem as being in counseling, the perspective of the youth is often very different from that of the clinician. In an institutional setting, for example, the daily life of the institution may be the most pressing issues for the youth. For example, concerns about receiving packages, the relative fairness or unfairness of staff, and so on, may dominate the thinking of the confined person. While the counselor may acknowledge the validity of these issues, the counselor desires to focus instead upon "real" issues such as personality characteristics, anger management, thinking errors, and the like.

Problems Which Both
the Clinician and the Youth Define

It is perhaps in this area in which the real work of counseling can take place. In family systems therapy, this area is defined as "joining" the youth. Here, both the counselor and the youth agree upon that the problem exists and agree to work to resolve it. This, of course, is the ideal in counseling. And it is one not often initially achieved with aggressive and resistant youth. For, as explained above, the youth's perception of the problem is often far different than that of the counselor. In fact, perhaps placed in the same situation, the counselor might not act in a way much different from that seen by the youth. Social psychological research has consistently demonstrated that we give environmental forces far too little credit for the actual force that they play in determining behavior. So, if somehow put in the same situation, the counselor may also not experience the behavior as being problematic.

But, of course, the counselor, hopefully, is not in the same situation as the aggressive and resistant youth. It is unlikely that the youth will soon change environmental circumstances in a manner that will result in significant change of attitude. And it is unlikely that that the attitude of the youth will change on it's own. So, it is left to the counselor to be flexible. The counselor, of course, cannot adopt the attitude and biases of the youth. To do so is to lose boundaries and effectiveness. Over-identification with youth does happen and never results in positive counseling outcomes. But the creative counselor can seek to find mutual areas of agreement and define counseling goals in terms of the common ground discovered. For example, both the counselor and the youth can share a goal of the person obtaining both a satisfactory release and being able to stay out of the criminal justice system after that release. Rather than addressing head on the maladaptive behaviors of the resistive youth, the counselor can attempt to "reframe" the problem in a manner that is agreeable to both. To illustrate, the counselor can attempt to have the youth identify "bad habits" that lead to reincarceration. The counselor might even acknowledge that the behaviors were once adaptive. For example, an abused youth needs to look at the world in terms of possible threat. For the world is, in fact, quite dangerous to that youth. To act in a manner which suggests any differently is not only foolish but also potentially suicidal. But, if the youth leaves that dangerous environment, then those styles of perception and interpretation are no longer adaptive. But, as we know, old cognitive habits and styles do not easily go away. If the counselor simply challenges them, or worse, labels them as negative without attempting to understand the adaptive function that they once held, then counseling will go nowhere. If instead, the counselor is able to reframe the thinking styles as being once necessary, but now as unproductive habits, then the youth may feel less threatened and more willing to explore alternative ways of looking at things.

Problems Not Seen by Either
the Counselor or the Youth

There, are of course, those potentially very difficult areas in which neither the counselor or the youth sees the problem. An easily understandable example would be when an youth is HIV positive but neither the youth nor the counselor knows this situation. Some types of problems are benign but others, as in the case of HIV/AIDS, are most certainly not. It is important in the case of aggressive and resistant youth that the nonmedical therapist have a basic understanding of those physical factors which may result in behavioral changes. Ideally, the counselor should make active use of medical consultation, when it is available.

THE TRUST/CONTROL DICHOTOMY

When workers are forced into a control role over the involuntary youth, another fundamental difference between working with voluntary and resistive youth arises—the trust/control dichotomy In the case of voluntary youth, the general circumstances are those of high trust and low control. Counselors really have no contingencies, no controls over the person seen in voluntary, outpatient work. The youth may choose to listen and follow the heeding of the clinician or they may choose not to do as was suggested. The clinician cannot force this on the voluntary youth, instead, the youth learns to trust and not fear counselors and to act on the suggestions out of that relationship. Again, this is the model under which most of our therapies have been devised. But in the case of the confined population, such as in a locked or secure residential treatment setting, we have generally the reverse situation: counselors don't fully trust the youth and they do not fully trust counselors. In certain circumstances, counselors may have a considerable degree of control over what residential youth consider to be the most vital aspects of their lives: from day-to-day privileges to the ultimate question of discharge. Counselors are caught in a role conflict between that of therapist and supervisor, even keeper. In such circumstances it should be expected that youth will try to manipulate counselors. And that may be perfectly natural. We all try to influence those who control us in some measure. It is important that counselors see this for what it is—sometimes a natural response to the unnatural circumstance of being in a locked treatment setting, but sometimes an expression of an antisocial or delinquent personality.

Counselors should remember, as well, that psychotherapy/counseling outcome research no longer focuses upon the question of what works, but rather on the questions: what interventions by what type of clinician work for what type of problem which what type of youth? (Davis and Brodsky, 1992).

THE PROBLEM OF THE MENTAL
HEALTH CURE ALL

Counselors must also remember that counseling and psychotherapy approaches per se cannot resolve all of problems of a given youth. For example, there is no evidence that traditional mental health interventions can "cure" antisocial behavior. We have some beginning evidence that specialized "thinking errors" or other cognitively based interventions have some impact upon antisocial behavior. However, these approaches differ significantly from the techniques generally taught in graduate programs in psychology, social work and counseling. The mental health staff member who attempts to use "traditional" methods is likely to experience frustration, failure and likely disillusionment. The youth, treated only with traditional mental health counseling, is likely, when he or she again breaks the law, to do so with a smile, feeling good about himself or herself and with a clear self-identity.

TECHNIQUES OF INTERVENTION
WITH THE UNWILLING YOUTH

Not surprisingly, unwilling youth are often not very verbal in their first therapy sessions. The therapist is likely to encounter angry, silent youth. Silence or denial, especially in the initial interviews, acts as a source of power on the part of the youth, who is, in actuality, a frightened, maladaptively functioning person who acutely perceives a loss of control in his or her life. To terminate such a person from therapy quickly is a reactive response to recalcitrance, and may prematurely end a process that might be, if the clinician is both patient and creative enough, successfully resolved.

The Prometheus Principle

Sometimes, denial and resistance are initially natural responses and to counter them, workers can use other natural phenomenon. For one, people are fascinated with themselves. One technique is that of objective self-awareness that signifies in effect, that when youth become observers of themselves they can become both fascinated and motivated. Too often, workers have removed the youth from discussions about them, kept knowledge from them, and as a result, reinforced the youth' sense of alienation, separation and resistance. When this happens, it increases, rather than decreases denial and resistance. One can, in these circumstances, utilize Brodsky's concept of the Prometheus Principle (Davis and Brodsky, 1992). Prometheus was the bringer of fire and light to the earth in Greek mythology. Share as much information as one can with youth. Within appropriate ethical constraints, share with them tapes, clinical records, and videos of themselves, and have them sit in on discussions about their psychodynamics and therapy. This can lead to fascinating discussions about themselves, in which they may well take the role of primary presenter.

In another illustration, the author was once confronted with a youth that had endured many, many annual psychological evaluations. In each of them, he was described as being resistant, defensive, and without insight. When the examination began, he was asked about this and he replied that he felt that most psychological explanations for his behavior totally missed the mark. The examiner tried a different tactic. Recalling the quotation of George Kelly: "When you want to know why a person did something, the best way to find out is to simply ask him," the examiner invited the youth to write his own section of the psychological evaluation. The examiner could write the first half and the youth could then read and respond to the thoughts of the examiner. The caveat was that both the examiner and the youth had to sign the report and therefore take responsibility for the contents. The youth eagerly participated. The results of his response to the examination proved to be fruitful topics of discussion in counseling. He began to enthusiastically participate in the very sessions he had, for many months, actively sought to avoid.

What is seen sometimes as resistance is actually boredom. Not all of us are verbal, abstract, and philosophical. Many of our youth are practical, and concrete—doers not talkers. It may be a bit personally threatening to contemplate, but perhaps some therapy sessions are not all that interesting. Youth need to leave the session with something, no matter how small it may seem. They can be taught specific skills such as anger management, stress management, assertiveness, and so forth. Allowing them to choose goes a long way toward reducing resistance and enabling counselors to introduce other topics.

Paradoxical Approaches

At times, active resistance to treatment can be the therapist's greatest ally. It takes considerable energy on the part of the youth to resist therapy. Rather than focus on countering that resistance, channel it to facilitate therapy. Recall the *Taoist* wisdom that the strongest tree in a storm is the willow, for it bends with the wind.

Counselors should strive to avoid becoming caught up in direct opposition and conflict with youth. Workers should move with the resistance rather than fight against it. Aim for second order change, a paradoxical response, so that youth embrace in an oppositional way the view the clinician originally wanted. Ask them why should they change. Instruct paranoid persons not to trust, telling them to go slow. With the denying and resistive youth, the most unsettling thing for them can be to have someone else (counselors) occupying the same cognitive space as they. All of this does not have to be deadly serious, as well. In fact, sometimes the language of change can be that of humor.

Therapy as Punishment

In that light, for truly resistive youth, individual work can be considered as an aversive contingency for inappropriate behavior. That is, if a therapist has youth that truly dread individual work but are willing to go to group, then if they participate meaningfully, they can avoid the noxious experience of clinician's office.

The Repentant Robber

Some time back, there was an individual who robbed a bank. He was not a professional bank robber. But he was an alcoholic. Apparently, one evening near Christmas, he became quite intoxicated and stumbled into a bank. There, he convinced a teller that he had a weapon and managed to steal a few hundred dollars. He made it successfully to his apartment and fell in his bed to sleep off his intoxication. When he awoke the next morning, he not only had a hangover, but also realized what he had done the day before in the bank. He was petrified. Not knowing what else to do, and after having a drink to brace himself, he called the police. He explained to them that he had become intoxicated, robbed a bank, and now wanted to turn himself in, hoping that he would not get into serious trouble. He was, in fact, quite lucky. He was shortly brought to trial and continued to apologize, this time to the court, for his illegal behavior. The judge took pity upon him and placed him on probation, with the condition that he check into a local hospital for alcohol rehabilitation. He did so dutifully, and while there also had a few other matters taken care of, such as gall bladder surgery.

Shortly after his release from the hospital, he fell off of the wagon. One day, after a particularly intense episode of binge drinking, he again found himself making an unauthorized bank withdrawal. This time, however, he did not make it back to his apartment, but was instead arrested during his abortive attempt at larceny. Sobering up in the county jail, he soon came to the conclusion that the judge would likely not have much of a sense of humor about this most recent turn of events. He correctly reasoned that he was in real danger of going to prison as a result of this last robbery.

Unable to find any other excuse for his behavior, he began to concoct an even better story. After a hanging attempt that was notable for considerable advance publicity, the jail psychiatrist saw him. He told the new and impressionable clinician that he was the "victim" of a terrible miscarriage of justice. He told the incredulous psychiatrist that when he had been treated in the inpatient alcohol drug detoxification program, that he had undergone surgery for the removal of his gall bladder. While under anesthesia, the "evil hospital doctors" implanted an electrical device in his head. The purpose of this device was of course, to conduct a particularly nefarious experiment to see what would happen psychologically to a honest man (him) who was forced to commit a crime (the bank robbery). Thus, it was not his fault that he had resumed drinking and subsequently attempted to rob yet another bank. Instead, it was all the doings of those "evil doctors." Since this was the case, how could he be punished for robbing a bank when it was truly the responsibility of the "experimenters?" How fair, indeed, would it be to send him to prison for a crime that, if he had not had that device in his ear, he would not have committed?

The psychiatrist, amazingly, agreed with him on the last part of this story. The psychiatrist believed him to be delusional and therefore, not responsible for his actions. The psychiatrist wrote a report that then became the basis for a successful insanity defense. The "reluctant robber" was then sent to the forensic psychiatric hospital.

Not surprisingly, as soon as he entered the hospital, he began to look for ways to be discharged. The treatment team, again not surprisingly, could find no true symptoms of psychosis. Instead, they saw him as an alcoholic and determined that he should attend and successfully complete substance abuse treatment prior any thought of discharge.

He hated substance abuse groups. He saw himself as not having a drinking problem (and if he did have one in the past, he had resolved it without the help of the hospital). But, he knew that if he simply refused to go to groups, that by the rules of the hospital, he would lose the privileges that he had managed to accumulate. Most important to him, he would not be able to go outside in the hospital courtyard and smoke cigarettes. He had to find a way to avoid going to groups without being seen as actively and deliberately refusing them.

He decided that what had worked in the past for him would likely work again. It was not his fault that he did not attend the groups, he was merely a "victim" of yet another "evil experiment." When the time came for group, he would eagerly arise with the other patients and head in the direction of the group room. But, just before he came close to the door, he would grab his ears with both hands and let out a loud shriek. Then, he would argue mightily with unseen persons who were ordering him to not go to the group. "No, No," he would yell. "I must go to the groups, I need the treatment. You cannot kill me just for going. Let me go, I beg you." He would shake, roll around on the floor, and even sob loudly at times. But, he would never go to the group. And, each time when confronted by the team, he would tearfully tell them that he truly wanted to go to the group. He knew that he needed treatment, but those "damn evil doctors in my head" were telling him that if he did go to groups that he would be killed. He was told, he said, that he was part of yet another experiment to see if he could cure himself. Thus, it really wasn't his fault, he really wanted to go to substance abuse group, but if he did, he would be killed. How could the team blame him?

He held the team hostage in this circumstance for a few weeks. I was called in to consult with the team. There was one thing that he hated more than going to substance abuse groups. It was meeting with me. For some reason, I did not buy any of his stories and had told him in direct terms that I thought he was doing a masterful job of manipulating others and avoiding personal responsibility. (At such times, he would generally grasp his head and moan. . . . and I would join in.) Thus, individual therapy with me was, perhaps, the most noxious of all experiences for him.

Knowing that substance abuse groups rather than individual sessions (especially with both of us grabbing our heads and moaning) were the treatment of choice, we designed a contract. If he would agree to go to groups, no matter what he said about hearing the voices of the "evil doctors," then he could avoid that which he detested the most: individual sessions with me. But, if he, for any reason—especially because of the "damn doctors"—he missed a session, he would receive a punishment. That punishment, of course, would be an individual psychotherapy session with me.

To my great embarrassment, he became an active and enthusiastic participant in substance abuse group. It seemed that he would attend anything to avoid seeing me individually. To my even greater embarrassment, he began to drop his resistance and was able to truly successfully complete the program.

The psychiatrist on the team was duly impressed. He, too, was an "evil doctor." But, of course, as his unwitting colleague, I was the victim. He gleefully told the story of my "cure" in various staff meetings and encouraged other teams to contact me. Soon, I was besieged with any number of referrals to "not work" with various resistant patients.

To use oneself as a punishment can be more than a small threat to one's professional self-image, yet it can and has been shown to be effective. To be successful in this approach requires that the therapist is aware of his or her own needs in the therapeutic process. Workers are generally socially oriented, wanting and needing interpersonal contact and closeness. But the resistive youth often frustrates those needs. That frustration then shows itself in therapy.

The Three-Session Minimum

Empowering youth with the choice to terminate therapy is an another suggestion, but it should not be offered in the first, second, or even third session. The research on psychotherapy outcomes indicates that there is little relationship between first session events and eventual outcome. A strong relationship was found between third session events and outcome, by that time, youth had become involved. Setting up contracts, even trial therapy periods can be tried but, above all, the first three or four sessions should be in place before the choice of termination is offered.

During the first three sessions, counselors should pay attention not only to what the youth say but how they say it, what words they use. It is much easier for workers to adapt to their language than they to ours. Is the therapist really sure that the words he or she is using are really understood? What is sometimes seen as resistance is nonunderstanding. In the other direction, if one begins to hear the youth using some of the therapist's words, this might be a sign of decreasing denial. This process is termed convergence, and suggests mutuality of language as one of the true markers of a facilitative counseling relationship.

The Saving Proportion

As workers attend to language, they should attend as well to their own interpersonal processes. This is especially vital with the resistive youth. Referring again to psychotherapy outcome research, some of the most significant factors in negative psychotherapy outcomes are generally the personal qualities of the therapist. One significant quality is the inability of the clinician to allow the youth to experience failure and learn from his or her mistakes. This latter concept can be assessed as one's "Saving Proportion." The more the therapist "protects" the youth, the poorer the outcome. Persons need to learn by, not be sheltered from life's experiences. Perhaps the most important technical errors of technique seen in negative-outcome psychotherapy were those that avoided attending to the interpersonal transaction between the therapist and the youth. To facilitate a positive outcome, one must not ignore problematic aspects of the youth's behavior, attitudes and participation. Further, one's interventions must be active, properly timed, and positive. If the youth seems noninvolved, or uninterested, the issue should be used readily as a focus, either directly or by means of paradoxical interventions.

THE THERAPIST'S EXPECTATIONS

A final consideration to think about concerning the resistive and reluctant youth is the danger of the self-fulfilling prophecy. No matter what we as counselors, would like to think we are simply not able to predict the future. Although it is most certainly true that the best predictor of future behavior is past behavior, we simply cannot be aware of all the potential influences upon a person to the degree that we can, with any reasonable degree of scientific certainty predict that behavior. Further, we must be careful about the labels we place upon our youth, especially youth. We tend to live up to what we perceive to be other's expectations of our behavior, and our youth are no different.

If we do not expect them to grow and change, then they will not. If we do not see them as human beings capable of growth, affirmation, and reconciliation, then neither will they. And if we do not see them, fundamentally, as fellow members of our society with rights, privileges, responsibilities and value, then neither will they.

PITFALLS

Counselors should not ignore dangerousness. Youth revelation of dangerous plans is often a cry for help. It is frequently seen that counselors are anxious about the violence potential of their youth and react to that by consciously or unconsciously denying the real potential for violence.

At the same time, counselors must not over-react. When at all possible, they should not place themselves in an adversarial role. When this must happen, the clinician must clearly explain the basis for their actions, be ready to process it with the youth at some later date.

Staff characteristics that increase violence: overstructured, authoritarian, inflexible attitudes. Inconsistencies in behaviors and consequences also contribute significantly to violence. Fearful staff produces fearful youth and, accordingly, increases the likelihood of violence. Staff characteristics that reduce violence: fair minded toughness combined with sensitivity and caring.

In this final section, we shall turn to forensic and legal questions that often accompany aggressive and violent youth. Until recent times, there was a great separation in the manner in which the law addressed violent juveniles and adults. However, today, we see an increasing criminalization of juvenile justice and a far greater number of youth being "waived" or "bound over" for trial in the adult system. For this reason, we shall in the forthcoming chapter, discuss forensic issues such as competency to stand trial and insanity.

Chapter 11

Forensic Psychological Aspects of Care

Much madness is divinest sense
To a discerning eye;
Much sense the starkest madness.
'T is the majority
In this, as all, prevails.
Assent, and you are sane;
Demur,—and you're straightway dangerous,
And handled with a chain.

Emily Dickinson
????

In 1982, Judge David Brazelon, describing himself as a "disappointed lover," chastised psychologists for overreaching in opinion formation and providing judgments that have ventured beyond scientific expertise into the province of those designated by society to make moral judgments. In the field, itself, especially following the Hinkley and Dan White case, the profession of mental health has debated within itself its place within the legal system. Moreover, as well, following well-publicized cases, public outcry about "bought experts" has often resulted in legislative response. As such, in the Federal system, experts no longer make conclusionary statements and in many states, the criteria for a not guilty by reason of insanity verdict was significantly tightened by removing the "irresistible impulse test."

Yet, the two professions are inextricably linked as both deal with human behavior. It is not so much which behaviors that cause the tension between the professions but, rather, fundamental conceptual differences for the ever-present strain.

TRAINING DIFFERENCES

Attorneys are trained in one language and mental health professionals in another. Yet, in the courtroom, both must communicate with each other. For example, in the "product test" in which it is asked if the act is a "product of a mental disease or defect." What is defined as "product" of mental illness to the law and to behavioral sciences is vastly different. Further, the term "mental disease or defect" in the law is narrowly defined, but for counselors, is nebulous concept, at best.

OUR LIMITED ART

The law often asks us to say that which we in mental health often do not know; and we frequently agree to try. Even in our most basic assessments, those of gross diagnosis of disorder, it is not uncommon for disagreement. What one clinician may see as schizophrenia, another may see as a mood disorder or even the result of a personality disorder. While this may be not an important issue within the clinic, when one clinician after another is paraded upon the witness stand in open court, fertile ground for folly results. Beyond looking foolish, we can, in fact, cause great harm. Lastly, we often are asked to be Solomon like and, tickled to the very core of our ego, agree. And so, as has been the case, we may attempt to answer, in a divorce case, whether one week or two visitation per year matters in relative impact upon a child. Or, is a man competent to be executed (which this author was once asked to evaluate and refused).

FREE WILL VERSUS DETERMINISM

The law assumes we act out of choice. Rewards or consequences then follow. Certain aspects of the behavioral sciences such as the psychodynamic assume, however, that all behavior is unconsciously motivated and deterministic in nature. In this model, we are never truly able to choose how we behave. If a mental health professional subscribes to this view, how then could that professional support that any criminal behavior is willfully chosen? Does that mean that no one person is responsible for his or her actions? Or, to use a more current model, many mental health professionals are of the opinion that certain aspects of behavior do, in fact, result from choice, but that other aspects are determined by a mix of environmental and unconscious variables. In a courtroom setting, when the question of culpability is asked in a yes or no manner, how can a mental health clinician answer such a question? How then, can difference be resolved?

THE MYSTIFYING NATURE OF TRUTH

In the behavioral sciences, we are told nothing is absolute. We are inherently probabilistic in our understanding while in the law, decisions become dichotomous and absolute. Further, the law is idiographic, to borrow the model of Allport, while the sciences are nomothetic in the study of individuals. To translate, the court is interested in the person, not how the person compares. Lastly, with all of our trappings, couched in scientific lingo and clinical mumbo jumbo, we sound far better, more truly accomplished then we, in fact, are. And some of us venture into the courtroom without even bothering to learn of the facts. What is, for example, the standard for competency? What does the average clinician know about predatory rapists beyond what is gleaned from the news and episodic journal articles?

THE CRIMINALIZATION OF JUVENILE JUSTICE: THE INCREASING ROLE OF FORENSIC PRACTICE IN JUVENILE COURTS

Susan Rotenberg the Executive Director of the National Coalition for the mentally ill in the criminal justice system wrote in her 1992 prologue to the monograph *Responding to the Mental Health Needs of Youth in the Juvenile Justice System*, that "perhaps the only system that is in worse shape than education or health care is criminal justice." Since, as we discussed in an earlier chapter, juveniles commit a significant proportion of violent crime; the stresses on the juvenile justice system are enormous. This pressure is expected to grow with the anticipated increase in the number of youth. It is estimated that the population of the United States between the ages of fourteen and seventeen is projected to grow from 13.2 million in 1990 to 15.3 million in the year 2000. Thus, if this trend does happen, the demands upon the juvenile justice system will far outstrip its already limited capacity. This is especially troubling, for as pointed out in Chapter 2, it is estimated that between 20 and 60 percent of the youth in the juvenile justice system suffer from an emotional disability.

A great part of the reason for this problem, beyond the larger social issues of course, is the conflicted nature and mission of juvenile courts. Early juvenile courts took the role of *parens patrie* or the "benevolent parent." Youth were seen as in need of direction and guidance. The focus was upon re-socializing and training youth. Thus, the terms "reformatories" or "industrial schools." Sadly, of course, these noble aims were never truly realized. Now, as juvenile crime continues to increase, the direction of juvenile courts across the country has increasingly turned to punishing and confining youth that violate the law. This re-focusing is also the result of the assertions of the 1960s by the United States Supreme Court that the juvenile courts were essentially unable to meet the demand of safeguarding the child and the community. The court decisions of *Kent*[1] and *Gault*[2] as well as others essentially stated that the constitutional rights of children were sacrificed in order to meet an unattainable goal of beneficial treatment in the juvenile justice system. As a result, the courts began to provide youth with a number of due process rights once reserved for the adult system. As the juvenile justice system has become more and more like the adult system, these due process questions have become increasingly applicable to youth in the juvenile justice system. As a result, forensic examinations that are much like those performed on adult offenders are increasingly being provided to juvenile courts.

This leads to a number of questions in the law. First of all, the definition of mental illness. Most states, including Ohio, use the same definition (O.R.C. 5122.01 (A)) of mental illness for both juveniles and adults. A very few states, such as Oklahoma and Virginia have attempted to develop special categories for juveniles suffering from mental disabilities, but trend is neither clear nor widespread.

A variety of circumstances have arisen in the juvenile justice system in which specific forensic evaluations may take place. These are (a) the assessment of violence risk or dangerousness and need for emergency confinement or treatment; (b) issues such as competency and criminal responsibility; (c) bind-over or waiver to the adult system; and (d) dispositional and treatment planning.

We shall explore each of these questions, bearing (once again) in mind that far more research is available in reference to adults than to juveniles.

WAIVER/BINDOVER OF JUVENILES TO ADULT COURTS

Often in serious felony cases, or with repeated crimes, the issue of the defendant's fitness for treatment in juvenile court is raised. The prosecution generally does this but some defendants may raise the question in the hopes that they may serve less time in the adult system. General assessment guidelines tend to take into account the prior criminal record of the youth, the seriousness of the offense, response to past treatment efforts and the present treatment resources afforded within the juvenile justice system. Issues of public safety are also considered in the determination.

Recently, many states have significantly changed those youth that would be bound over into adult court. These laws often mandate that certain violent or repeat juvenile youth must be sent to adult prisons and take away much of the discretion which was once left to the juvenile court. The result of this change is that many more youth are incarcerated in adult correctional system with a corresponding decrease in youth held in juvenile facilities. For the forensic counselor, these youth held in adult settings present very difficult problems. They often have very long sentences. One sixteen-year-old youth examined by the author was serving a thirty-five to life sentence in an adult prison, for example.

The Case of Richard:
A Sixteen-Year-Old Murderer

> Richard, a sixteen-year-old, white male, was evaluated for the purpose of determining treatment and intervention options to assist in controlling his violent behavior. At the time that he was seen, he was in an adult prison, serving a thirty-five to life sentence for the aggravated murder of his foster father, whom

he had beaten to death with a sledgehammer. He had been in the foster home, his twenty-second, for only one day when he snuck up behind the foster father, knocked him unconscious with the hammer and then attacked the foster mother with the same hammer. The foster mother lived but was severely brain-injured. The youth was apprehended two days later by police after he had stolen their car and driven to another state. He was pulled over for driving the wrong way on a one-way street. A check of the license plate identified it as being stolen and he was eventually charged with Aggravated Murder and Felonious Assault. The juvenile court waived its jurisdiction. He plead guilty and was sentenced to the adult correctional system.

Since he was admitted to the adult system, he was then placed in a reception unit pod that contained over 300 adult male felons. Shortly afterward, he attempted suicide and was placed in the prison mental health unit. He then became extremely violent with attacks upon both other inmates and prison staff. He was eventually placed in solitary confinement.

Records indicated that he was the youngest of nine children from an extremely problematic family characterized by substance abuse, physical abuse, and neglect and mental illness. All of the children had been removed and were in the custody of various child welfare agencies and treatment facilities. He was diagnosed as hyperactive in the second grade and became involved in the juvenile justice system at age ten. His first out-of-home placement took place at age four and he experienced multiple foster home placements since that time. He was placed in juvenile correctional facilities at age twelve following an attempt to burn down his foster home. At age thirteen, he attempted to stab a youth with the sharpened end of a toothbrush. His juvenile court record subsequently contained charges of attacks upon others, attempting to strangle another child, arson, and carrying a concealed weapon. Assaultive behaviors, self-mutilation, escape and suicidal threats were frequent throughout his various placements. Clinically, he was seen as Attention Deficit Hyperactive Disorder, and a severe Conduct Disorder. No evidence of psychosis was ever reported.Intellectually, he consistently presented within the borderline range of general intelligence.

In the examination, he was found to report an extensive history of physical abuse victimization. He also claimed that he had been sexually abused by at least one foster parent and by a series of older youth in various placements where he had resided. He stated that he eventually began perpetrating against other youth, generally forcing them to perform oral sex. He reported as, well, an extensive history of substance abuse beginning at age nine. He described his temper control problems as "I just lose it." He claimed to often not remember what he did. He said that he did not recall much of the events of the crime for which he was imprisoned. He stated that he had no idea why he attacked the family, stating, "I had just gotten there. I didn't even know them." He said that when he saw what he did, "I got scared and took the car. I didn't know what I was doing." He said that his arrest and trial were "a blur." He said that when he arrived in prison, he was frightened of the other prisoners and was afraid that he would be raped. He claimed to hear the voice of the foster father who had allegedly raped him telling him that he was "no good" and "should die." He could give no reasons why he should live and presented with a picture of hopelessness and anger. At the time of consultation, he was on constant suicide watch and would not contract with staff to not hurt himself. He was subsequently sent to the prison system psychiatric hospital, where he stayed briefly and then was released to a special unit that had been developed to house persons under eighteen who had been sentence to the adult prison system. Shortly after his transfer, adult inmates who broke into the unit murdered another youth.

COMPETENCY TO STAND TRIAL

Throughout the law, the concept of "competency" is infused. One must be, and is presumed competent to enter into contracts, to testify, to stand trial, to enter pleas, and to be punished. The most frequently adjudicated issue, however is that of competency to stand trial.

Competency to stand trial has its roots in English Common Law. During the times of the Crusades, it would sometimes be the case that a Lord would be tried in absentia in order to take away his land.

Resultantly, it was decided that it was unfair to try a person *corpus en absentia*; later this concept was expanded to include being mentally present at a trial. It is also thought that during the seventeenth century, when defendants would stand mute before the Bar that the British jurors would then be forced to determine if the person was mute by "malice" or "by visitation of God." This was originally aimed to address the deaf and mute defendant but later was expanded to include the "lunatic." American jurisprudence, in its heavy reliance upon English Law has used the concept of competency since the very beginning of the nation. In 1835, a man accused of attempting to murder President Andrew Jackson was declared unfit to stand trial. In both the British and American model, competency has three primary objectives:

1. That the trial will result in accurate results
2. To assure the proceedings will be dignified
3. That imposition of punishment will be morally justified

Juvenile Courts and Competency to Stand Trial

Traditionally, all juveniles brought to trial have been presumed to be incompetent simply because of their status of juveniles. When the juvenile court operated under a rehabilitative, welfare of the child model, this was not seen as problematic. However, as juvenile courts have become more like adult courts, due process questions such as competency have been addressed in a number of states. Frost (1997) reported that twelve states and the District of Columbia currently have specific provisions for competency examinations and restoration to competency for juveniles. While many of these statutes parallel the language used in adult courts, the time allowed for restoration may be somewhat shorter. This is especially problematic since much of what data that does exists suggest that youth who are examined tend to be found significantly lacking in the skills and abilities required for competence. As juvenile courts continue to become more like adult courts and as more youth are bound over to the adult system, this issue becomes especially important. Cooper (1997) found, to illustrate this point, examined the factual understanding about trial of 112 youth ages eleven through sixteen. The majority did not have adequate knowledge. When exposed to some basic training, their general knowledge level did increase but not to the degree required for actual competency to stand trial. In this group, as in others, special care was warranted for both youth under thirteen and those of limited intellectual abilities. Similarly, Heilbrunner et al (1997) examined the single case of a ten-year-old boy who was diagnosed with both attention deficit hyperactivity disorder and learning disabilities. As pointed out by the authors of this study, the functional aspects of competency are unique to juveniles. Further, it is of vital importance to separate out the effects of developmentally caused deficits from those caused by psychopathology or mental retardation.

There is a dearth of research on competency to stand trial for juveniles. Grisso (1987) pointed this neglect out over ten years ago. Currently, the Institute of Law and Public Policy at the University of Virginia is conducting a research project on the Adjudicative Competence and Maturity in Juvenile Delinquents. This study examines the competency of seventy-five juveniles ages ten to fourteen and seventy-five juveniles ages fifteen to eighteen. A second generation of research is developing comparative data on a sample of seventy-five incarcerated adults and seventy-five psychiatrically hospitalized youth. It is hoped that this research will provide measures for assessment of competency for youth.

When competency is considered for youth, it must be addressed within the developmental context of the youth. This is especially vital in terms of cognitive and emotional functioning and cultural issues. Youth are not simply smaller versions of adults. As should be recalled from Chapter 2, they differ both qualitatively and quantitatively in their cognitive and emotional processes. Young adolescents differ substantially from older adolescents in their ability for abstract reasoning and emotional maturity. Adolescents show tremendous variations in social maturity and independence. In some cases, the youth may be easily lead or influenced by a person perceived by the youth as being significant admirable. Other youth may suffer from disorders such as Oppositional Defiant Disorder or Attention Deficit Hyperactivity Disorder. These disorders can result in difficult or resistive behavior that is a consequence of the disorder rather than a specific choice. However, the clinician that is unfamiliar with adolescence may misinterpret the behavior as simple unwillingness. For example, a youth who may have been traumatized in some fashion and suffer from Post Traumatic Stress Disorder may manifest thinking or behavioral patterns unique to PTSD adolescents. If unrecognized by a forensic examiner unfamiliar with these disorders, true impairment could be misperceived as well.

Using the Developmental Matrix of Table 1 as a guide, it is clear that cognitive and emotional development follows specific sequences. While the age ranges in the figure are approximate, it must also be held in mind that many youth that are traumatized are "frozen" developmentally at a particular stage. Thus, the youth who suffers from early trauma will likely think in a very concrete, egocentric manner, have diffuse and dyscontrolled emotions and, especially, have significant issues with trust versus mistrust. Abused youth, as well, may have considerable issues concerning shame, doubt, self-valuing and self-blame. They may not have developed a sense of personal identity and may be quite alienated and isolated. The examiner who assesses competency in youth must compare the functional requirements of competency with the developmental skills and abilities of the youth in question. It is for this reason that competency assessments of youth must be performed by clinicians that are adequately trained in both forensic issues and child and adolescent development.

Current Formulations of Competency

Dusky v. *United States*, 362 U.S. 402 (1960)[3] establishes the current definition of Competency that is generally applied to both adults and adolescents. The Supreme Court held that "the test must be whether he (the defendant) has sufficient present ability to consult with his attorney with a reasonable degree of rational understanding and a rational as well as factual understandings of the proceedings against him."

Note that the focus is upon the *present* condition of the defendant rather than a retrospective analysis of his condition at the time of the alleged offense. Secondly, the issue is upon the *capacity* of the person to cooperate with counsel rather than the person's willingness. Lastly, a *reasonable* degree of understanding is required rather than a total or complete understanding. Thus, the threshold for competency is not high. Competency consists of five basic elements. They are detailed below.

Knowledge of the Present Charge

The youth should be aware of what he or she is charged with. This does not require, of course that the youth are able to cite the exact legal code. However, the youth should have a general and correct understanding of what he or she is accused of doing.

Knowledge of the Possible Consequences

The youth should be aware of what could possible happen if convicted. This, of course, must include the possibility of transfer to the adult criminal justice system. Knowledge is more than mere rote recitation of the possible outcomes. Knowing requires being able to apply that knowledge to the unique, personal situation of the youth.

Ability To Have an Appropriate Relationship with an Attorney

Beyond the gross issues of psychopathology such as paranoid delusions that might prevent effective relations with counsel, the examiner must be aware of the social and emotional development of the youth. Some youth, especially traumatized youth, may not be able to trust anyone. Other youth, especially those from differing cultures, may be unable to effectively relate with the attorney. Others youth may be so overwhelmed that they will simply do what an attorney tells them to do. While this may be advantageous in certain cases, attorneys who represent youth will want to be assured that the youth can make informed decisions. Note that this requirement speaks to ability rather than willingness to relate. The determination of this difference requires considerable understanding of adolescent psychology.

Knowledge of Courtroom Procedures

It is, of course, not required that the youth have as much knowledge as the attorney does. The object is not for the youth to know enough to pass the bar. Rather, the youth must have a basic familiarity with the adversarial nature of court (especially due to recent trends in the criminalization of juvenile court). The youth must also be aware of those types of behaviors that might be self-damaging.

The Capacity to Integrate and Efficiently Utilize Knowledge and Abilities in Either a Trial or Plea Bargaining Situation

Although much of the assessment of competency has traditionally focused upon trial, the reality of the justice system is far different. Most cases are decided by some sort of plea arrangement prior to any trial. The youth must be able to make informed and rational choices in such matters. As well, the choices are often made quickly and under pressure. Adolescents who have limited problem solving and reasoning capacities may attempt to look as if they understand the situation when they, in fact, do not. The examiner who focuses only on the "high school civics" aspect of competency and neglects the reality of the court processes may then ignore the essential qualities required for competency in the unique circumstances faced by the youth.

Psychosis and Competency

In the case of both youth and adults, psychosis does not automatically equate with incompetence. A psychotic defendant who can satisfy the above conditions may, thus, be found competent. Competency may be raised at any point in the adjudication process, although it is most often raised by the defense. The issue of competency is always a legal, not a clinical issue. Competency issues have been used to stall or delay legal processes and have been, in the past, abused. Competency has been misused to lengthen detention of persons who were perceived as community problems. In *Jackson v. Indiana* 406 U.S. 715 (1972), the Supreme court decided that Jackson, a deaf mute could not be indefinitely committed to a mental hospital, that such a commitment violated constitutional guarantees of equal protection and due process. Resultantly, limits were placed on to what facility and for how long an incompetent defendant may be committed for treatment. Further, if the person was not restored to competency, the charges would be dismissed and disposition of the case would take place via civil rather than criminal processes. Although strides were made with *Jackson*, it remains the case that persons civilly committed as unlikely to be restored to competency on serious charges likely remain hospitalized for significant periods. This is often the case because hospital staff are unwilling to risk the release of such "criminal" defendants/patients.

Amnesia

While it would initially seem that amnesia would be per se grounds for incompetence, that is not the case. Amnesia is difficult to challenge and is often found in cases of severe, dissociative violence. In the case of *Wilson* v. *United States* 129 App. D.C. 107, 391, F.2d 460 (1968), it was determined that Wilson, who suffered a fractured skull during a police chase, could be tried if the amnesia did not preclude his ability to consult with his attorney using information supplied by the prosecutor to reconstruct the case.

Drug-Induced Competency

The most common treatment intervention for competency restoration is that of psychotropic drugs. Courts consistently recognized the drug treated defendant as competent. However, at times, the artificially imposed tranquillity of the patient may work against a successful insanity plea. Further, the patient may attempt to refuse medication. In such matters, the right of the individual to refuse potentially harmful drugs is contrasted against the right of the state to bring the person to justice. Although most states do not allow the incompetent patient to refuse medication, the issue remains unresolved especially in the case of juveniles.

Characteristics of Incompetent Defendants

Research concerning Incompetent defendants (Steadman, 1979; Davis, 1986) found adult incompetent defendants to generally exhibit a high degree of general psychopathology who are often representative of "marginal individuals" with limited general life skills. Davis (1986) also found that non-restored individuals, not surprisingly, had greater degrees of adaptive deficiencies than persons who were restored did.

Quality of Competency Evaluations

The primary variable in quality of evaluations rests more with the examiner's understanding of the referral question and the competency standard than the clinical difficulties presented. Untrained examiners often confuse psychosis and incompetence. However, with trained examiners, this is not the case. Rather, competency evaluations are comparatively "easy" evaluations in most cases since the question is functional and present oriented. In support of this, research indicates that high reliability is generally found between trained examiners. The question of validity is more complex is less clear as judges rarely challenge expert opinions and there is no independent criterion.

Competency Instruments

As the question is functional and specific to a particular situation, there is no true "competency test." Those that have been developed fail to meet standards of reliability and validity accepted for psychometrics. There are certain structured interviews such as the *Interdisciplinary Fitness Interview* (Roesch and Golding, 1980) and the *Competency Assessment Instrument* McGarry, 1973). Which have been found to useful structuring devices for the clinical examination. There is to date no specific instrument for assessing competency of juveniles. However, Grisso and his colleagues at the McArthur Foundation are working to remedy this current situation. The following case presents a clinical example of a competency examination.

Example Competency Examination

• REFERRAL INFORMATION

Mr. CST is a 15-year-old, single, African-American, male referred for evaluation of competency to stand trial by Juvenile Court. His defense counsel is the County Public Defender's Office.

Mr. CST is currently charged with one count of Assault (2303.3) (M-1) and Criminal Trespassing (2311.21) (M-4) as a result of an alleged incident that took place on XX/XX/9X in the XXX Shopping Mall. He has remained in the Detention Center since that time.

• EVALUATION PROCEDURE

Mr. CST was evaluated in the County Detention Center II for a period of 1.0 hours. The conditions of interview were adequate. In addition to the interview, the arrest reports were reviewed. Mr. CST was informed as to the nature and objectives of the evaluation, and that the findings would be submitted to court. As such, the material would not be confidential. He appeared to understand these circumstances but due to his mental status was confused to the degree that he was unable to sign the appropriate documentation indicating this understanding.

• SOURCES OF INFORMATION

The following sources of information were utilized in the preparation of this report:

1. Telephone Consultation with his attorney
2. Review of Police Reports concerning the alleged incident.
3. Interview of Mr. CST on XX/XX/9X for a period of approximately one-hour.
4. Interview of his foster parents.
5. Review of Children's Services Records.
6. Telephone Interview with his caseworker
7. Telephone Consultation with his Guardian Ad Litem

• BACKGROUND INFORMATION

The available records and interview with the youth indicate that he was born on XX/XX/XX in this city. Mr. CST was quite disjointed in his thinking which also appeared to be influenced by paranoid delusions and hallucinations. As such, he is not seen as being a reliable source of personal information. Therefore, the following data must be viewed with caution and should be confirmed by additional sources, as well. Further, due to his paranoid processes, he was highly guarded in revealing details of his life. It is assessed that this guardedness was due to his mental illness, rather than a willful attempt at deception or evasive. In that Mr. CST was actively paranoid and delusional during the recitation of his history, these likely delusional beliefs are related in the history as examples of his psychotic thought processes.

Mr. CST claimed that he never knew his parents and that he was "born in a foster home." He described his upbringing in negative terms and described it as "rough." He claimed that he was frequently moved from foster home to foster home and that, at age eleven to a group home. He stated that he stayed in the group home until he was fifteen. He denied any history of developmental delays, and serious childhood illnesses, but stated that he was struck in the head with a baseball bat when he was age six and lost consciousness. However, he was not taken to a hospital. He claimed, in beliefs which rapidly were colored by delusions, that he lost his memory "many times" and had to "get thought training" at a hospital (the name of which he could not recall) and that since that time, he has been "scattered." He denied any other history of serious illness. He denied present physical illnesses, as well and stated that he is not taking any medication.

He could not provide a coherent account of his educational history. When asked about schooling, he replied "some kind of skitter-scatter. Somebody Pranking, it was not too healthy." He claimed that he "is out of them" but could not describe how he was discharged.

• MENTAL STATUS EXAMINATION

Upon evaluation, this youth appeared to be an African-American male who appeared to be his stated age. His hygiene and grooming were much less than adequate and he had a marked body odor. His gait and posture were non-remarkable. There were no overt indications of gross or fine motor dysfunction. His speech was normal in variable in tone with episodic hostility, variable in pacing and normal in volume. There were marked and overt indications of loosening of associations, disjointed thinking, idiosyncratic speech and tangentialness. As well, he was often vague, rambling and circumstantial in his thinking. These features are typically seen with severe mental illnesses, especially those of the schizophrenic spectrum. There were no indications of and flight of ideas. His level of psychomotor activity was non-remarkable. His eye contact was direct and his attention span was poor. His manner of social interaction was guarded, distant and marginally cooperative.

This youth presented labile (highly changeable) affect that varied from neutral to angry. He claimed a mood which was mixed because "of all of the memory scatter." He appeared to be actively delusional. To illustrate, in describing his childhood, he stated that in the foster home, "they almost killed me twice. I have been dead twice. Just by child abuse. Things have been going on since childhood, some kind of abuse computer or fire drill computer. The foster home people killed me one time in a tornado. I was just an infant. Then I got thrown in a freezer and my neck got broke. I got brought back to life. I don't know how. The foster home people were taking my money reading my thoughts. Just about everybody tries to hurt me. They try to kill me. It is mind control. They stole my thoughts. They scattered people out via the privacy act." These illustrations appear to indicate paranoid delusions as well as delusions of thought control and thought stealing, again, symptoms often seen with the schizophrenic disorders. He appeared, as well to have a history of hearing voices and also appeared to be actively hallucinating. When inquired if he had any unusual experiences or heard voices, he replied, "That's what up with this so-called scatter, you can send radio signals to and from people, especially through the so called Netcare channels. You can hear people thinking and talking about me. I hear it in the cell, some kind of military thing. They are scatter trying to read my thoughts and take my money. Now these people are going through my memory. I can hear them over the intercom. They are with the government. So people think I am crazy, but I am not. I'm just working my job. The people got me in the situation, they said they are gonna try to take my clothes and make me live in so-called houses." He denied current depression as well as any disturbances in his sleep, health or appetite. He did not appear to be anhedonic. He denied any history of suicidal behavior. He denied present thoughts of harming himself or others. There were no clinical indications of specific phobias, obsessions or compulsions. He was oriented to time, place and person. Due to his rambling and disjointed thinking, it was not possible to formally test his memory functions. As well, it was not possible to formally test his abstract reasoning or judgment. His insight and judgment appeared to be substantially impaired.

• COLLATERAL HISTORY

Interview with the foster parents of the youth indicate that he had been recently placed in their foster home upon being released from an intensive care locked residential treatment facility. (Records were requested from that facility but have not yet been received by the examiner.) He has only been in the foster home for about two weeks. He currently takes Haldol, a powerful anti-psychotic medication that is prescribed for him by the outpatient department of the residential treatment center. At the foster home, his behavior has been unpredictable and bizarre. He is observed to eat trash, he is withdrawn and often speaks non-sensibly. The Children's Services caseworker stated that this youth was born to a patient in a state psychiatric hospital and it is believed that his father was also a patient. The mother has a long history of schizophrenia. He has been in seventeen out of home placements since birth. He has become progressively more bizarre and idiosyncratic. He was placed in the residential center due to an episode of attempting to have sex with a dog. The Guardian Ad Litem verified the history of the youth given by the caseworker.

• DIAGNOSTIC IMPRESSION

As noted earlier, Mr. CST was not seen as being a reliable historian and much of his personal data was obtained through outside sources. What is clear is that he appears to presently be actively psychotic. It is further clear that he has a family history of mental illness and has an extensive number of previous out of home placements. These factors have resulted in serious disruption in his overall adaptive functioning. Currently, he is too mentally ill to accurately assess his intellectual functioning. Many of his symptoms appear to be those of schizophrenia, especially that of the paranoid type. The probability of a schizophrenic disorder is especially supported by the family history of mental illness. However, since his psychosis is presently of such an acute state, it is not fully possible to either administer psychological tests or fully interview this youth. As such, only a provisional diagnosis can be made. On the basis of the above-cited data, the following diagnostic impression is offered:

Axis I:	(298.9) Psychotic Disorder, Not Otherwise Specified
Axis II:	Deferred Rule out Borderline Intellectual Functioning
Axis III:	Deferred
Axis IV:	Psychosocial Stressors: Involvement in Legal System
Axis V:	GAF+25 (current)

• UNDERSTANDING OF CURRENT LEGAL SITUATION

Due to this individual's mental status, it was quite difficult to formally assess his knowledge of court processes. Utilizing the McGarry Competency Assessment Instrument, a structured assessment of functional characteristics associated with fitness for trial, this youth was found to not be able to demonstrate an adequate understanding of legal defenses available to him. He refused to discuss the various plea options stating "There are no charges against me." He has exhibited behavior, according to his attorney (such as refusing to speak with her) which would suggest that he would be unmanageable in the court as a result of his mental illness. Further, he appears to be paranoid and agitated and this may well be seen in the courtroom. Due to his paranoid delusions, thought disorder and agitation, he cannot adequately and rationally relate to his attorney. He refused to accept that he has an attorney, since he believes that he has no charges against him. Clearly, as well, due to his mental illness, he cannot rationally participate in the planning of legal strategy. It was not possible to assess if he is adequately aware of the roles and functions of major courtroom personnel, however this seems likely from the materials discussed. It is not possible to assess, for the same reasons, his understanding of court procedure. He does not, as a result of his paranoid delusions appreciate the charges against him and the possible consequences. Further, he presently does not have a realistic appraisal of his circumstances. Essentially, he stated that he was approached by the mall security and "He spinal tapped me. I was the one giving the spinal tap. They were using the government against me." Due to his mental illness, he lacks the capacity to disclose to counsel his version of the alleged offense nor can he relevantly and challenge witnesses. He appears to be realistically self-serving, in the legal sense.

• CLINICAL FORMULATION

Based upon the results of this examination, it would appear that Mr. CST is a seriously mentally ill individual, who most probably suffers from some form of schizophrenia. However, due to the inability to perform a comprehensive psychological evaluation, this diagnosis cannot be formally made. There is also the possibility of substance abuse. Although his claims of abuse may be delusional, if true, then a diagnosis of post traumatic stress disorder could also be considered. Intellectually, it was not possible to assess his functioning.

• FORENSIC CONCLUSION

In conclusion, it is my opinion, within reasonable scientific certainty, that Mr. CST is mentally ill. Because of his illness, which is of currently psychotic proportions, he is not presently capable of understanding the nature and objectives of the proceedings against him, nor can he assist his attorney in his defense. Clinically, he is assessed as being not competent to stand trial.

He is currently in immediate need of psychiatric hospitalization. There is a substantial probability that he could be restored to competency within the time period allowed by law. Due to his serious mental illness, the charges against him and his current clinical presentation of agitation and paranoia, the most appropriate and least restrictive treatment setting would be that of a psychiatric hospital.

As a result of this report, he was found to be not competent to stand trial. He was placed in a psychiatric hospital where he was given a diagnosis of schizophrenia. He was treated with anti-psychotic medications and eventually restored to competency. He then entered a plea of guilty and was returned to the residential treatment center.

VICTIM TRAUMA AND THE WITNESS DISCLOSURE PROCESS IN CHILD ABUSE

The reporting of child sexual abuse allegations has risen dramatically in the past decade. The majority of these allegations are found to be substantiated. However, increasing attention is now being given to those few children who either deliberately, or in an attempt to please others, provide false testimony of sexual abuse. In such circumstances, the effect on the accused can be devastating. Even when the allegations are cleared, the individual may remain under suspicion, or suffer from psychological trauma.

Case Example 1: Deborah

Deborah is a fifteen-year-old female whose parents were divorced when she was three years old. She has had no contact with her father. At the age of three, she was diagnosed as evidencing Attention Deficit Hyperactivity Disorder and was unsuccessfully treated with medication. Her behavior at that time was described as oppositional and highly conflictual with peers. Her adjustment to school was poor and her behavioral problems escalated. Her mother and she were involved in various counseling programs but there was no substantial change in her behavior. By the age of twelve, she had become involved in truancy from home and school and was suspected of substance abuse. When she was thirteen years old, her mother remarried to Tom. He had not been previously married and attempted to establish himself in the "father" role in the new family. His attempts to either establish a positive relationship with his stepdaughter or assist in discipline were unsuccessful. One year after the marriage, Deborah stated to a school guidance counselor that her stepfather had been touching her in "private places" and had forced her to perform oral sex on him. A report was filed with the children's service agency and an investigation was begun. Despite the stepfather's and mother's strong denial, as well as the previous behavioral problems of the youth, the allegation of abuse was substantiated and a finding of probable cause was made. Charges were filed against the stepfather. He was unable to post a bond and was placed in jail. After three months, Deborah recanted her story and indicated that she had lied to "get him out of the house." The stepfather returned home and family counseling was begun. Deborah continued to act out and was eventually placed in a residential treatment center.

Case Example 2: James

James is one of three brothers who were allegedly molested by his older cousin who had lived with the family for one year. James was six years old and was referred for evaluation as to his competency to be a witness. Clinically, he was seen as of normal intelligence but presented with severe anxiety, hyperactivity, hypersensitivity, and symptoms of posttraumatic stress disorder. When the investigators had raised the possibility of testifying in court, he became highly upset and ran from the interview office.

The issue of victim trauma recollection as it pertains to child sexual abuse is a complex one and involves not only the psychological effects of the trauma, itself, but questions as to the competency of the child to be a witness; the reliability of recall of the alleged event; and lastly, the possibility of simulation or malingering.

Competency of Children to Testify

As indicated in Benedek (1993), the mental health professional who must evaluate the competency of a child of testify is faced with several important questions:

1. Is the child competent to testify?
2. What data from the child are admissible?
3. How can the child be prepared for the experience of testimony?
4. Can courtroom procedures be modified for testimony?

Competency is a legal term that addresses the ability to perform a certain task. Generally, the question addresses certain basic factors such as the capacity to observe, intelligence, memory, communication ability, appreciation of differences between truth and falsehood and the understanding of the need to be truthful in such situations.

Competency and credibility (truthfulness) are separate issues. Competency is determined by a judge as to the above-cited functional capacities. Truthfulness is determined by a judge or jury based upon evidence presented in a hearing or trial.

The question of competency has its roots in common law and focused upon the insane, the mentally deficient and children. Children below a certain age were generally barred from providing testimony.

However, as early as 1770, in the English case *Rex v. Braiser* (11 Leach 199, 168 Eng Rep. 202, 1779),[4] it was held that there is no arbitrary age below which children are unable to testify. In the United States, in 1895, the United States Supreme Court (*Wheeler v. United States* [159 US 523, 1985])[5] upheld a trial court determination that a five-year-old child was competent to testify in a murder trial.

In 1975, the Federal courts adopted new Rules of Evidence. Prior to 1975, the majority of states held by either case law or statue that children below a certain age were presumed incompetent to testify. This age varied from ten to fourteen years old. Below that age, a hearing was held to determine the testimonial capacity of the child. In the 1975 revision, the grounds of incompetence were narrowed in rule 601 that stated "Every person is competent to be a witness except as provided otherwise in these rules." In so doing, the Federal courts curtailed the need for an automatic hearing of competency but continued to give the trial court judge discretion to hold a hearing if there was reasonable concern as to the competence of the child witness. Competency hearings remain common for children under the age of ten.

The legal standards for competency are essentially the same in most legal jurisdictions. The courts assess whether or not a child has the ability to perceive, recall and relate his or her experiences accurately and has the difference between truth and falsehoods. Currently, in the United States laws concerning the competency of child witnesses fall into four areas. In some states, the federal rules are followed and a large majority of children are found to be competent. In the second area, certain states have laws that state that the child is incompetent unless it can be shown that the child understands the meaning of a taking of an oath. The purpose of the oath, in modern times, is to assure that the witness fully understands the seriousness of the proceedings and the duty to tell the truth. In the third case, some states have a presumption that children below a certain age are incompetent to testify unless the trial judge determines that they are able to testify. In the states following this approach, the great majority of youth over the age of five are found competent. A fourth and a new trend is legislation which permits children of any age to testify in matters of alleged sexual abuse.

Beyond the above-cited evaluations of developmental readiness, it has become far more common to have children evaluated to determine if any mental problems impair the child's ability to serve as a witness in a trial does.

EYEWITNESS TESTIMONY AND VICTIM RECALL

In recent years, the scientific study of memory has been an important adjunct to the courts. The courts base the findings often upon the validity of persons' ability to recall objectively specific facts. However, the study of memory suggests that, often, we do not, in fact recall events exactly as they occurred, nor is there an objective way to determine if a memory is correct. As is the case with competency, there is really no sound body of research concerning juveniles and eyewitness testimony. That which is known is generally extrapolated from studies of adult memory. While much useful information can be suggested, it is again the case that the developmental status of the youth has likely considerable impact upon the youth's ability to recall eyewitness testimony. Further the younger the witness, the more susceptible that youth is to influence by a person perceived as being of higher status. With this caution in mind, the following is a brief review of what has been learned about adult eyewitness testimony.

Research Concerning Eyewitness Testimony

Studies divide memory into three stages: acquisition, retention and retrieval. Acquisition is the encoding of information into memory. Retention is the storage over time of the memory and retrieval is the ability of the individual to access what happened. There are many factors that interfere with each of these processes.

When a complex event takes place, it is impossible to attend to, much less remember every detail of an incident. If a detail is only glimpsed, then the persons' expectations may distort what is seen. Thus, even at an early stage, a totally complete and accurate representation of the event is unlikely. Thus, a person may see a stick and recall a gun. Finally, during the retrieval stage, the conditions of recall may influence what is remembered.

Acquisition Factors

The length of time in which an event takes place has a great impact. The longer the exposure, then in general, the more accurate the recall. However, persons do not accurately recall how long events take place and often make systematic errors in estimating how long ago events occurred. The frequency of events also impacts upon recall. However, novel one-time events, such as abuse, are frequently recalled accurately.

The core event versus peripheral details. Witnesses are more likely to recall the core or central event than details. Thus, the actions rather than the features of the person are more likely remembered. Recall of details is poorer with violent rather than nonviolent incidents. Accuracy of core events and peripheral details appears unrelated.

Expectations. The persons' expectation of what is to be recalled also has great influence. Persons tend to recall better details linked to that which is expected to be recalled. However, in fast moving, ambiguous circumstances expectations may lead to misperceptions and inaccuracies in recall.

Violence and stress. Recall performance peaks at moderate stress (Yerkes-Dodson Law), thus under high arousal the range of attention is narrowed to the point that relevant details may be ignored. Even though the range of memories may be limited, those details recalled by victims of stress tend to be accurate.

Retention. Retention is the second stage of memory. During the retention interval, encoded information may be affected by various factors. The length of time that passes between an event and its attempted report can lead to forgetting. In addition, information learned *after* the event can distort the original memory.

One of the most well documented findings in memory research is that forgetting increases with time, although familiar material is generally lost more slowly. However, it has been shown that certain types of memories, such as stranger recognition are more influenced by the amount of attention given during encoding rather than just the simple passage of time. However, even these memories will fade somewhat.

Malleability of memory. The work of Elizabeth Loftus and her colleagues has demonstrated that through the use of misleading or directive questioning, subjects can drastically change their purported recall of events. Witnesses can be made to report such things as barns that were not seen, incorrect colors of hair and even location of headache pain. Terms such as *the car smashing into the other* can influence the recall of the alleged speed of a car versus the use of the term *the car hitting the other.* If the subject is under high stress or if the questioner appears to be of high status or trustworthiness, misleading information is more likely to be accepted.

In summary, memory can suffer during the retention interval due to either forgetting and/or contamination by misleading information. But this is not always certain. Memory that is familiar or central or very well encoded is more resistant. The credibility of the questioner can also be of great influence. In addition, subjects who were warned that questions might be of a distorting nature were found to be less influenced and if the questions follow the order of the remembered events, distortion is also less likely.

Retrieval

It has been shown that the most effective interview technique is to allow first a total free recall, then ask open-ended questions and lastly to ask specific questions. When a subject is introduced as a suspect, recall can be significantly influenced. Subtle and non-subtle environmental factors may also reduce the accuracy of retrieval. The closer the context of the retrieval is to the event, the better the recall (why "lineups" are more accurate than "mug shots." Cross-racial face recognition is much more difficult than same race. However, the more cultural familiarity the witness has, the greater the likelihood of successful identification. Improper lineup techniques (having only one obvious suspect) can also decrease accuracy. Conscious and unconscious resistance (simply being tired) can also have an effect. Lastly, disguises or changes in physical appearance can also reduce effective recall.

CRIMINAL RESPONSIBILITY AND JUVENILE COURTS

In criminal law, the defendant is presumed to have the capacity, or "free will" to choose whether to commit a crime. If there is no free will or *mens rea*, then there can be no crime. To illustrate, if a person accidentally runs over another, without intent, he or she cannot be charged with murder, although civil penalties remain possible. Similarly, if the defendant is, due to mental defect or disease, unable to form criminal intent, then no crime can be charged.

The defense is quite misperceived. It is rarely raised, generally less than 1 percent of all criminal cases enter an insanity (NGRI) plea. In most cases, it is unsuccessful. In Ohio, currently, there is less than 500 persons committed to either hospital or community settings due to insanity findings while the number of persons incarcerated in prison soars above 20,000. Persons found insane tend to be incarcerated at least as long as those sent to prison. NGRI patients have been found slightly less dangerous or about the same as felons convicted of the same crime.

Juvenile Courts and Insanity Defenses

In the past, the concept of a not guilty by reason of insanity plea was seen as unneeded in juvenile courts. If the mission of the court was the welfare of the child, then there was no concept of "criminal" responsibility. However, in recent years, the situation has drastically changed. Some juvenile court jurisdictions have utilized the plea option in special cases (for example, the case related in the chapter on juvenile homicides). However, an increasingly far more common trend is that of waiver or bind-over to the adult system. In such cases, the insanity plea is then entered in the adult court.

Standards

In that the use of the insanity defense in juvenile courts is still uncommon, it is generally the case that adult standards are utilized in some fashion in juvenile courts. While this approach may, on the face, have merit, there are still substantial concerns. Specifically, little research data exists to assist in separating out what might be effects of developmental differences between results of a mental illness. Secondly, psychopathology in youth does not always manifest in the same manner as in adults. Symptoms vary in both quality and intensity. Thus it is paramount in any examination of sanity that the examiner be experienced in the psychopathology of adolescents as well as normal adolescent development.

Historical Background

The test of insanity has its formal roots back to Daniel M'Naghten who killed the private secretary of Sir Robert Peel in a 1842 murder attempt. The M'Naghten Rule is as follows:

> At the time of committing the act, the party accused was laboring under such a defect of reason of the mind, as not to know the nature and quality of the act he was doing, or if he did know it, he did not know he was doing what was wrong.

Following criticism of this rule due to its rigidity, American courts adopted a second prong, the "Irresistible Impulse Test." In this model, a person is innocent when he cannot control his urges, even if he understands the act to be wrong. Because he cannot control himself, he is seen as lacking free will and is not responsible for his actions.

In Durham, the court expanded the "product test," partially in response to criticism of the M'Naghten standard (*Durham v. United States* 214 F.2s 862, 873-74 (DC Cir. 1954)). It stated that:

> An accused is not criminally responsible if his unlawful act was the produce of a mental disease or defect.

However, this model was vague and almost totally uninterpretable. In place of the product test, a new model was drafted with attempted to provide specific guidelines, yet not be as rigid as the previous efforts. The American Law Institute Standard states:

> A person is not responsible for criminal conduct if at the time of such conduct as a result of mental illness or defect, he lacks substantial capacity either to appreciate the criminality of his conduct or to conform his conduct to the requirements of law.

The following case reports detail various aspects of the insanity defense. In the following case, the concept of "wrongfulness" is illustrated. As will be seen the young adult described in this case was clearly so impaired by his illness that he could not understand the wrongfulness of his actions.

The Case of the Man Who Believed in Doubles

Peter was a quite, withdrawn but highly intelligent youth. An only child, his parents were much older than he was. He had few friends and spent most of his time either studying mathematics or books about war. As soon as he graduated from high school, he joined the Navy. There, he excelled in technical areas and eventually received specialized training in nuclear warfare. This was, for him, the greatest achievement one could have. His family had always served in the military and he was carrying on the proud tradition.

However, it seemed as if the pressures of the service were too much for him. He withdrew even more and began to act in ways so unusual that his superiors eventually referred him for a psychiatric examination. He was found by the psychiatrist to be in the first stages of a schizophrenic process. Given a medical discharge, he was sent home. This was completely unacceptable to him, after all of his training and family tradition, this simply could not be happening.

At home, he withdrew deeper and deeper into his isolation. He began to lose the boundaries between reality and his private thoughts. Eventually, he developed the delusional belief that he had never really been discharged from the Navy. Instead, he was home on a "special intelligence assignment." But he could not understand why this had happened. Until one day, when he was eating dinner with his parents. He noticed that they seemed to be acting somehow differently, but he could not pinpoint exactly why.

He remained awake for the next few days and nights, trying to understand what was so very different about them. Then, early one morning, he realized: the two people living with him were not really his parents. They were, in fact, Russian Agents. Somehow, the KGB had cleverly managed to place nearly exact doubles of his parents with him! But why? Clearly, it was because of his special training with the Navy. These two spies obviously had the mission of tricking him into talking about his service and revealing military secrets.

Once he realized what was happening, his duty became clear. As a member of the Armed Services, he was obligated to stop this espionage. That night, while his parents were sleeping, he took a large, heavy metal vase and beat them both to death.

Once he fulfilled his mission, he then did what any sailor must do. He reported his actions by driving to another state, entering a military base and reporting to the military police his successful "mission."

He was subsequently found to be not guilty by reason of insanity on the basis that his delusional belief that "doubles" had been switched for his parents (or Capgras Syndrome) prevented him from being able to see his actions were wrong. Instead, on the basis of his delusions, his actions were not only lawful, but also laudable.

This individual was originally, found incompetent to stand trial and hospitalized. During the first portion of his hospitalization, he continued to believe that his victims were "spies" and not his parents. Eventually, as his hospitalization progressed, he came to understand that he had, in fact, killed his parents. At that point, he became highly suicidal. When he was eventually restored to competency, he entered a plea of not guilty by reason of insanity. The court found that he was at the time of the act suffering from a paranoid delusion that caused him to believe that he was "doing his sworn duty to defend the country" and was, therefore, not criminally responsible for his actions. He was, accordingly, found not guilty by reason of insanity and placed in a psychiatric hospital, where he remains.

A much more difficult consideration is the person who is both truly mentally ill and able to understand the wrongfulness of his or her actions. In the past, many of these individuals were found to be not guilty by reason of insanity on the basis of "irresistible impulse." This prong of the insanity test suggested that while the person was able to *cognitively* understand the wrongfulness of the act, he or she could not restrain himself from acting. Informally, the test was known as "The Policeman at the Elbow" test. That is, would the person still complete the act if a police officer were standing nearby? Some individuals, such as persons experiencing a manic episode are completely unable to control their impulses. In such cases, such persons would be found not guilty by reason of insanity. However, in many states, this consideration was removed as a basis of an insanity plea, leaving only the more rigid "knowledge test," generally a modified version of M'Naghten. The result, therefore, is that a number of persons who were once hospitalized as not guilty by reason of insanity are now found guilty and incarcerated in correctional facilities.

The following case of another young adult illustrates the complexities of persons who are both mentally ill and are able to understand the wrongfulness of their actions. Such cases are often extremely difficult for the examiner in that the person clearly is mentally ill, but by legal standards, is also responsible.

The Case of George

George is a twenty-two-year-old male who entered a plea of not guilty by reason of insanity on a charge of Aggravated Murder. He was alleged to have stabbed his wife to death in front of his nine-year-old daughter. There appeared to be no question that he was a seriously mentally ill person both prior to the offense, most likely during and after it. The question for the examiner was whether that mental illness prevented him from knowing the wrongfulness of his actions.

There were considerable historical and clinical data to support that he was seriously mentally ill. He had a documented history of mental health treatment, including prescription of anti-psychotic medication. He had clearly deteriorated in his adaptive functioning to the extent that he lost his job as a result of coming to work late because of an obsession to pick up road kill from the side of the highway. He had become isolated and seemed increasingly peculiar to those few people with whom he maintained contact.

In addition, following his arrest, he was taken to a state hospital where he stayed for a short period and was given the diagnosis of paranoid schizophrenia by the attending hospital staff. As a result, he was found not competent to stand trial and hospitalized for restoration to competency in a specialized forensic hospital. At this facility, as well, he was seen as mentally ill and given the diagnosis of paranoid schizophrenia. Eventually he was restored to competency and returned to court, where his attorneys entered a plea of not guilty by reason of insanity.

He was then examined for his sanity at the time of the offense using the M'Naghten Criteria. He claimed, by the time of the examination, nearly two years later, that he had killed his wife because he had heard messages from "helicopters." These helicopters told him that he was to take kill her and then he and his children would "go to heaven."

His crime was discovered when his wife, who had left him, was reported missing by friends. It was well known in the small community that she had filed for divorce and custody of the children. That day, she had gone to the house to pick up the children from their visit with George. When she did not return at the expected time, her family became concerned and called the police.

When they responded to George's house, the police found her body hidden under a tarp in his yard. When surrounded, he surrendered to the police. When the police entered his house, they noted that his clothes had been washed and the knife used as the murder weapon had been washed clean of blood. He was, however, nearly incoherent and was taken to the local mental health center. From there, he was placed in a psychiatric hospital and eventually found incompetent to stand trial.

In the analysis of his criminal responsibility on the basis of a not guilty by reason of insanity plea, the question was whether George, at the time of the commission of the offense, as a result of a severe mental disease or defect, did not know the wrongfulness of his acts. This criterion contains three concepts: (1) Severe Mental Illness; (2) Knowing and (3) Wrongfulness. Each of these shall be discussed separately.

Severe Mental Illness

It was clear from the evidence that George suffered from a long-standing mental illness. Evidence used to support this finding included the fact that George's mother had a long history of mental illness. In fact, it is reported that his mother has been diagnosed with Delusional Disorder, a diagnosis that has also been given to George in his contacts with mental health providers prior to the offense.

George also had demonstrated a clear deterioration in his adaptive functioning. As an adolescent, he completed high school. As a young adult, he served in the United States Army and received an honorable discharge. Following his discharge, he was initially able to secure employment and worked steadily. However, apparently as his mental illness progressed (gradual progression of symptoms and resultant deterioration is often seen in major mental illnesses), his ability to work became increasingly compromised. This deterioration continued to the extent that he not only lost his job, but also was brought by his employer to the mental health center. Such a deterioration is often characteristic of severe mental illnesses such as schizophrenia.

Members of his family, including his wife, expressed concern over his deterioration into mental illness and he was diagnosed at the County Mental Health Center as suffering from Delusional Disorder, although there was also initial concern about substance abuse involvement. He was seen in individual counseling and prescribed antipsychotic medication. George's diagnosis at County was that of Delusional Disorder, Paranoid Type. This disorder is characterized by non bizarre delusions in which the person believes that he or she is being conspired against, cheated, spied on, followed, poisoned or drugged, maliciously maligned, harassed or obstructed in the pursuit of long term goals." His clinical presentation, both at admission and throughout his treatment before the offense, was supportive of this diagnosis. That he did not see a need for treatment and eventually discontinued his sessions is a behavior often seen with severely mentally ill persons, especially paranoid individuals. By definition, persons with paranoid beliefs do not see themselves as being abnormal, but instead, see others as victimizers.

When admitted to a psychiatric hospital, he was given the same diagnoses. An MMPI-2 administered to him also supported the diagnosis of a paranoid psychosis, with marked elevations on scales 6 and 8 (paranoia and schizophrenia). Subsequent MMPI-2's given to him in the next two years also reflected this profile and further supported a finding of serious mental illness. Thus, when taken together, it was clear that he was a mentally ill person prior to the offense, most likely during the offense and most certainly afterwards.

Knowing

The second aspect of the criteria in a sanity examination is that of Knowing. Was George, because of a severe mental illness, unable to fully know the significance of his actions? On the other hand, more specifically, was he able to comprehend the nature or quality of his behavior as being criminal? While it is true that seriously mentally ill persons may have considerable difficulty reasoning in a rational manner, it is also true that they do not become so impaired that they lose touch with basic concepts such as the legal or moral correctness of an action. In this case, evidence taken from descriptions of his behavior supported that he did, in fact, know or appreciate that his actions were "wrong."

In the records of the case, it was noted that he made two statements to the police. In the first statement to the police, just after the murder, George stated that he was aware that the stabbing of his wife did cause her death. He repeated this knowledge to the mental health examiners at the County Mental Health Center and at the state hospital to which he was taken just after the crime. As such, in his initial statements, he clearly gave the impression that he was aware that the actions of stabbing her caused her death.

After a period of hospitalization and a series of hearings and conferences with his attorney, he modified his story a number of times. In the final version, given to the forensic examiner, he stated that he thought that she would be brought back to life. Because of this, he told the examiner, he did not think that he was really causing her any harm. Significantly, this version arises much later in the legal process and was thought to be likely untrue. As such, it was determined that he did, at the time of the offense, have the ability to "know" that his actions would cause the death of his wife.

Wrongfulness

The criteria of wrongfulness address two aspects. One is the simple knowledge that something is criminally wrong. That is, the action is a crime for which there are legal sanctions. The second aspect is potentially more abstract, recognizing the moral wrongfulness of his actions. A final aspect of this analysis is whether he is able to reason sufficiently to make this determination. In this regard, it is noted that when he made statements to the police, he said that he was aware that his actions were illegal. In his statement to the police, he indicated that he "was flipping out, I couldn't believe that I could do something like that in front of him."

Most importantly, the police discovered that he apparently washed off the knife. Further, he admitted in his second statement to the police that he lied to them the first time about the knife. He initially stated that it simply fell into the washing machine. However, in a later statement, he stated that "The knife didn't fall into the washer accidentally, I threw it in there to try to wash it off." Clearly, if a person attempts to eliminate evidence, the implication logically follows that he is aware that he may be prosecuted for the action. As such, attempts to evade detection are, in an of themselves, indications of knowledge of criminal and moral wrongfulness.

In his second statement to the police he stated, spontaneously, that "I just don't feel responsible because with all the poisons and the things that people were putting in my food and drink. My state of mind was completely out of order." In this instance, he appears to be justifying his behavior because of mental illness. This attempt fails on two counts. First, the act of justification implies knowledge of wrongfulness. Secondly, persons who are delusional and psychotic do not see themselves as insane. Rather, they see themselves as being justified in their actions. It appears clear that he made this last statement after he has returned to jail and became fully aware of his dire circumstances.

Because of the examination from which this case study was drawn, this person was found not meet the criteria of "not guilty by reason of insanity" at the time of the offense. He entered a plea of guilty to a lessor charge. He currently receives psychiatric services within the correctional system.

DIMINISHED CAPACITY

Although diminished capacity differs within jurisdictions, the general implication is that due to psychological disturbances or impairment, the defendant's capacity to form requisite intent, or *mens rea* was somehow affected or diminished. It may be an emotional or emotional disturbance or drug or alcohol intoxication that limited the defendant's capacity to form intent. Generally used when there is not sufficient support for an insanity plea, and often in cases of intoxication, this plea is controversial. In essence, the person's attorney postulates that although the person did commit the crime, he or she did not, in fact, intend to do so. Many states have no provision for this defense. However, the question may often be raised at the mitigation of sentence phase of the trial.

NGRI Disposition

Over the past few years, coupled with the tightening of standards for being found not guilty by reason of insanity, courts have also tightened their control over persons who have already been found NGRI. This is often in response to cases in which a person adjudicated NGRI was released into the community either by discharge or on some sort of pass status and committed another violent crime. Public outcry and considerable media attention often follow. Then, as a result, the laws governing the treatment of mentally ill offenders often are scrutinized.

The primary changes seen tend to be that the court must approve on grounds unsupervised privileges and that consideration of public safety is the principal factor in making commitment decisions. Persons held as NGRI, due to the *Jones v. United States* Supreme Court decision may be confined *longer* than minimum sentences since the court held that the basis of the confinement is not the offense but the mental illness. However, state legislative revisions that have not been constitutionally challenged often stipulate that the person may be held up to the *maximum* sentence, which in some cases, could be life.

Once again, in the case of juveniles, dispositional issues are unclear. If the finding of insanity was made by a juvenile court, then the authority of that court will typically end at the age of eighteen (or in some states may be extended to age twenty-one). Thereafter, however, the person is part of the adult system. Currently, there are no provisions for transfer of jurisdiction to the adult courts of those few youth found mentally ill as a juvenile. Typically, the only possible avenue is to attempt civil commitment under probate law standards. This, of course, is viable only if the youth continues to meet the standards for civil commitment.

Competency for Execution of Sentence

As noted in Benedek, (1992) The United States Supreme Court examined in the case of *Thomson v. Oklahoma* the constitutionality of the death penalty for person who committed the capital crime while under the age of sixteen. In *Thomson*, the major issue before the court was that of cruel and unusual punishment under the Eighth Amendment which was made applicable to the states by the Fourteenth Amendment. This decision prohibited execution of persons who committed the crime while under the age of sixteen. For persons over the age of sixteen, competency to be executed evaluations address issues of the persons understanding of why the sentence is being carried out, their ability to communicate with their attorney as well as the persons ability to settle final affairs. If the person is found incompetent, he or she may be remanded to a forensic hospital for treatment for purposes of restoration. Evaluations of this sort often result in considerable ethical issues for counselors. If the clinician does perform the evaluation, then the general questions of competency apply to this specific issue.

Mentally Ill Parolees

Another neglected area is that of mentally ill youth discharged from the juvenile justice system. Little is known and few programs exist for these specialized youth. In fact, their mental illness often makes them extremely difficult to be placed in community settings.

MALINGERING

Malingering is defined as the voluntary production or exaggeration of symptoms in order to obtain an identified goal. Typically, one encounters malingering in cases that have some sort of criminal or civil legal involvement. A person may malinger mental illness in order to avoid criminal responsibility for an offense or a person may malinger some type of disability to obtain insurance or disability payments, for example. Other circumstances might be malingering in order to obtain a desired or avoid an undesired placement (such as moving from a prison to a psychiatric hospital).

In *DSM IV,* malingering (V65.2) is defined as "the intentional production of false or grossly exaggerated physical or psychological symptoms motivated by external incentives such as avoiding military duty, avoiding work, obtaining financial compensation, evading criminal prosecution or obtaining drugs. Under some circumstances, malingering may represent adaptive behavior, for example feigning illness while a captive of the enemy during wartime. Malingering should be strongly suspected if any combination of the following is noted:

1. Medico legal context of presentation (e.g., the person is referred by an attorney to the clinician for examination).
2. Marked discrepancy between the person's claimed stress or disability and the objective findings.
3. Lack of cooperation during the diagnostic evaluation and in complying with the prescribed treatment regimen.
4. The presence of an Antisocial Personality Disorder.

The Case of Bruce: Malingering

Of course, not all persons who plead mental illness are actually mentally ill. Some persons will malinger or attempt to simulate mental illness.* The following case presents an individual who clearly understood the wrongfulness of his actions and attempted to portray himself as mentally ill to avoid legal consequences.

>   Bruce was a seventeen-year-old, African-American male, who on Christmas Eve, kidnapped, raped, and killed his high school teacher. He was bound over to the adult court and while awaiting trial in jail, allegedly attempted to hang himself in his cell. He was seen, as well, as being moderately paranoid, but without hallucinations. He was then transferred to a forensic hospital for further evaluation. Background data indicate that he was raised in an urban setting in a family disrupted by separation, alcohol abuse and physical abuse. He left school in the ninth grade after numerous behavioral problems. He became extensively involved in substance abuse. He was reported to have abused animals and frequently played with matches. He had a history of juvenile delinquency for theft and shooting at other inmates with a BB gun. He received no inpatient, outpatient, or residential mental health treatment.
>   Upon admission, he claimed to hear voices, one of which told him that he was God. He claimed to hear voices telling him to jump on others and to urinate on the floor. He claimed to be "chased by communist robots" and frequently told others that he committed the crime because the "communist robots told me to do her." He claimed to see faces on his bedroom wall that directed him to kill people. However, staff behavioral observations found him to frequently engage in conversation with other patients, that he would laugh, smile and frequently was seen as taking advantage of less functional patients by having them buy him commissary items. He was not observed to exhibit behaviors characteristic of patients who actually experience hallucinations.
>   On forensic psychological examination, he was given an MMPI that was found to be invalid and suggestive of malingering. The Rorschach, as well, was found to contain highly un-

---

The reader is referred to the works of Phillip Resnick and Richard Rogers for detailed discussions of malingering.

usual responses of a type not associated with psychotics and suggestive of deliberate simulation. While he was able to read the MMPI and, as well, complete sentences on the Rotter Incomplete Sentences Blank, he earned scores on the WAIS-R of verbal-58, performance-53, and full scale-53. The overall presentation was that of malingering.

The attending psychiatrist also held the assessment of malingering. The patient was discharged as competent to stand trial. He was found guilty of the offense and sentenced to a life term.

Factitious Disorder

Malingering should not be confused with Factitious Disorder, in which a person feigns illness but there are *not* external incentives. While it is the voluntary production of symptoms, the goal is to meet a psychological need of assuming a "patient" role and to receive some type of care. The production of symptoms is not otherwise understandable in view of the individuals life circumstances and there are no external incentives for the youth's behavior. Factitious Disorder presents with predominantly psychological signs and syndromes (300.16); with predominately physical signs and symptoms (300. 19); and a combination of psychological and physical symptoms (300.19).

Factitious Disorder by Proxy (Munchausen's Syndrome)

Another, fairly rare type but potentially quite dangerous type of Factitious Disorder was once known as *Munchausen's Syndrome*, named after Baron Von Munchausen, a reputed teller of exaggerated tales. The essential feature of this syndrome, described in the *DSM IV* section, *Criteria Sets and Axes Provided for Further Study*, is the deliberate production or feigning of physical or psychological symptoms in another person under the individual's care. In most cases, the victim is a young child and the perpetrator is the child's mother. It is important to note that external gains such as financial rewards or attainment of parental custody rights are *absent*. (In such cases, the behavior would be criminal in nature and most likely due to an Antisocial Personality.) In true Factious by Proxy cases, the person either simulates or induces the condition and then presents the victim to caretakers while denying any knowledge of the cause of the problem. Most often, gastrointestinal, genitourinary and central nervous system problems are reported. Claimed psychological conditions are relatively less frequent. Only the knowledge and sophistication of the perpetrator limit the intensity and severity of the claimed disorder. Cases of suffocation with a pillow to feign sleep apnea or SIDS, water intoxication and exposure to toxins are reported cases. In some circumstances, physical or sexual abuse is claimed. (Also, if unfounded, it must also be considered if these claims may also be the result of a delusional process and not deliberately produced.) The most common diagnostic sign is an atypical presentation of the claimed disorder of the victim as well as inconsistent diagnostic findings. As well, the perpetrator, even when despite sophisticated medical knowledge, may seem uncharacteristically unconcerned about the seriousness of the situation. Life stresses such as marital or financial difficulties may trigger the disorder. The perpetrator may act alone, but there are reported cases of both parents acting in concert. Factious by Proxy victims may suffer a significant morbidity and mortality risk and are also at risk for the development of Factitious Disorder, themselves. Perpetrators frequently, as well, may have a coexisting Factitious Disorder, which often is not evident while the perpetrator is inducing or simulating a disorder in the victim. When discovered, the perpetrators often become angry, depressed and suicidal. They may attempt to remove the victim from medical care and seek other providers.

Ganser Syndrome

Certain incarcerated offenders may manifest a seemingly malingered condition in which the prisoner appears to be stupefied and gives nonsensical, approximate answers to questions. Typical responses would be giving the date as January 35, or saying that 7 plus 7 is 77. Although some researchers have described the behavior as malingering, others describe it as a hysterical psychotic reaction to the stress of being incarcerated. It should not be automatically seen as evidence of malingering to avoid prosecution since it can be clearly ascertained that the symptoms arose after the person was put in jail. However, malingering should be ruled out in the case in which a person is being examined for competency to stand trial or could be sent to a more desirable placement (a hospital, for example). Symptoms may also be manufactured in an attempt to take a hostage or be moved to a facility more open to the possibility of escape. Lastly, some persons may evidence a Posttraumatic Stress Disorder like reaction to the totality of their crime and incarceration.

Potential Evidence of Malingering

As noted earlier, the primary criteria are a combination of external goals, an antisocial personality disorder and symptoms that do not fit known mental disorders. Malingerers tend to claim symptoms which are unlike those actually seen in psychotic individuals (e.g., such as a case in which a prisoner claimed to be controlled by a "green communist robot." They tend to overact such symptoms and in contrast to true psychotics attempt to call attention to their symptoms. As well, malingerers often claim a sudden onset of symptoms while, in fact, true psychotic illnesses generally develop over time. Additionally, their behavior, when viewed in total, does not usually conform to the claimed delusion. Malingerers are rarely sophisticated enough to be able to demonstrate the residual or negative symptoms of schizophrenia such as social impairment, blunted affect, concrete and disordered thinking. In the examination, malingerers often respond slowly to questions or will develop symptoms in response to indirect suggestions by the examiner. Lastly, a non-psychotic motivation is often fairly clear as an explanation of a malingerer's offense (Resnick, 1993).

Psychological testing, especially the MMPI-A can be highly useful in the diagnosis of malingering. Validity scales such as F, and F (b) are especially important, particularly when considered with other scales such as L, K, VRIN, and TRIN.

Another valuable method for the diagnosis of malingering is clinical observation. Malingerers are generally not able to keep up consistent feigning of symptoms for a prolonged period of time. Therefore transfer to a facility with twenty-four hour-trained observation is often critical.

It is much more difficult to identify malingering in cases of individuals who may have had actual mental illnesses in the past or actually mentally ill persons who exaggerate their symptoms.

Dissimulation

While most attention is directed to the problem of malingering, the behavior of dissimulation is often an extremely important question. Dissimulation is an attempt to minimize or deny symptoms. This is most often seen when a person is in a treatment setting and is seeking discharge or avoidance of certain treatments such as medication. An example would be a paranoid person who, after being found not guilty by reason of insanity and hospitalized for a violent crime, attempts to convince staff members that he has recovered and is no longer delusional. Clearly, such circumstances could pose considerable risk of safety to the community if a dangerous mentally ill person is inadvertently released from a hospital. Such cases have been the basis of many wrongful deaths and malpractice cases against hospitals and mental health professionals. Clues to dissimulation include the presence or history of a paranoid condition, an underlying personality disorder, rapid reduction of symptoms and sudden "insight." The youth may take on a "model" role and attend all prescribed treatments. Participation is generally superficial, however, and the youth frequently "cheeks" or otherwise does not actually take medication. Dissimulation must be differentiated from recovery from transient psychotic episodes, and recovery from substance induced psychotic episodes and mood swings.

Persons with a history of violence should always be seen by a noninvolved clinician or counselors for a second opinion prior to discharge. The MMPI-A may also be of value, particularly when L and K scales are elevated.

Chapter 12

Malpractice:
Regarding Each Other Testily

WORRYING ABOUT LITIGATION

Being sued is perhaps the single most cited fear of mental health professionals. In actuality, the feared litigation explosion does not exist (Brodsky et al., 1989). Further, when a clinician is sued, most often, the case will not be successful. But when a clinician is sued, the psychological cost can be quite significant.

MALPRACTICE DEFINED

Malpractice by definition means a wrongful, bad or inappropriate action by a professional. Professional recognition results in professional accountability. In legal theory there are many approaches to professional malpractice but most claims are based upon theory of negligence: that the professional failed to meet proper standards of care, thereby breaching the legal duty to the recipient of the services. There are certain essential elements of malpractice (Eagle and Kirkland, 1990):

1. A legal duty must exist between the practitioner and the injured party
2. The practitioner was derelict in that duty
3. That there was harm or injury of some sort
4. That the harm or injury was directly and proximately caused by the professional's dereliction of duty

Another distinction is that between errors of judgment and errors of fact (Resnick, 1995). To illustrate, the failure to obtain relevant data, such as prior records or laboratory tests, which contribute to an improper diagnosis would be an error in fact. In contrast, errors in judgment are not actionable when the clinician has acted in good faith and has exercised requisite care in obtaining necessary information and arriving at a diagnosis and treatment of the youth's condition. A clinician may make an error in judgment without falling below the usual standard of care.

Negligence

Negligence involves violation of a duty to provide adequate care. The duty is usually clear cut and easily defined-once the therapist accepts the youth. Alterations in relationship are more difficult and may raise significant questions. Most troublesome is termination. If termination not resolved therapeutically may raise issues of abandonment. Also, sexual relations would be clear violation of therapist duty.

Therapists are required to possess a reasonable degree of learning and skill common to their professions, exercise reasonable care and diligence in the application of those skills, exercise their best judgment in the application of those skills, render services based upon up to date information and conform their practices to methods approved by their profession.

The plaintiff must prove breach of duty. If the breach is established to have taken place, then it must be also shown that the action or omission was negligent that is it violated the duty of care owed by the practitioner. In most cases, this will require testimony by another professional.

If above is shown, then harm must be proven. If there is no harm, then there is no liability. Lastly, if there is harm, there most be proof that the harm was directly and proximately caused. That is, the harm was the direct and foreseeable result of the practitioner's negligent act or omission.

Standard of Care

The client has a right to expect services of the quality of the "typical professional." That is, that the professional is in the possession of and exercises the knowledge and skill common to the profession and remains abreast of recent scientific advances and elevates the quality of services within the bounds of reasonable expenditures and personal effort.

This does not mean that the professional must be flawless. Errors in judgments are not actionable if the clinician acts in good faith, had made sufficient inquiry and examination into the cause and nature of the disturbance, had exercised reasonable care in making the diagnosis and prescribing treatment and otherwise had not deviated from generally accepted standards and practices. However, the appropriate standard of care is increasingly no longer "community" but national standards.

Specialization brings with it greater risk. Professionals with specialized credentials are held to a higher standard of care.

Vicarious Liability

Clinical Supervisors hold the duty to the client. Even mental health professionals who employ but do not hold clinical supervision may be held liable. Team practice may, as well, hold liabilities if a team member ignores the duty to monitor the professional performance of other team members.

Governmental Immunity

Governmental Employees are rarely protected by immunity if found to be negligent. Increasingly, cases throughout the county have weakened any claim of immunity. Those clinicians working in public funded agencies are now, essentially, held to the same standards as private practitioners and persons who work in private, nonprofit agencies.

Avoidance and Defending Against Claims

    a. Remain aware of and conform to applicable standards of care.
    b. Communicate those standards to the youth and guardian. Provide for informed consent.
    c. Strive to assure conformity to standards by other team members.
    d. Provide a thorough assessment and diagnosis.

    e. Maintain complete contemporaneous written documentation of all aspects of care in every case. If documentation does not exist, do not recreate it and never alter documentation unless it is clearly shown as altered and dated as to when.

    f. Consider having either a witness or some form of recording with youth that are at risk.

    g. In release decisions, obtain a second opinion from a non-involved clinician whenever possible.

    h. In cases where there may be a duty to warn or breach confidentiality, seek consultation from both a colleague and an attorney. If necessary, go to court, assert confidentiality and be ordered to provide information.

    i. Practice good therapy and document it.

CONFIDENTIALITY

Confidentiality is the duty of the clinician to reveal information about no one unless required by law. Certain circumstances, such as alleged abuse of a child mandate the breaking of confidentiality and the reporting of the allegations. In general, however, confidentiality is protected. Of note is that the holder of the privilege is the parent or legal guardian, not the youth, or the clinician.

Lastly, it should also be noted that if a client does file a lawsuit against a mental health professional, then that professional is free to use confidential information in his or her defense.

DUTY TO WARN

According to common law in the United States, a person is not held responsible for the acts of another unless the person had a special relationship, such as a therapist-patient with the other. In order for such an action such as negligence to take place, it is generally held that some sort of duty is an essential element. In most jurisdictions, the existence of a duty depends upon the legal test of reasonable foreseeability. That is, would a reasonable and prudent person be likely to foresee some type of harm or injury as a result of the act or failure to act? Additionally, when a person, such as a psychotherapist holds special training and skills (and represents himself or herself as having those skills), then the law will demand that the therapist conduct him or herself in a manner consistent with that special knowledge. Further, a special responsibility is generally thought to exist only when one person agrees to assume responsibility for another. Thus, there is no special duty to control a person from preventing harm to another unless there is an agreed upon special relationship between the person with special skills and the potentially violent person or between the person with special skills and the potential victim. Typical examples would be prison wardens and directors of residential treatment centers for youth that serve as the custodians of the person.

As an illustration in Ohio law, as delineated in Littleton v. Good Samaritan Hospital, 39, OS (3d) 86, 529, NE (2d) 449 (1988),[6] such a special relationship was determined to be between a psychiatrist and his or her patient in a hospital setting. Liability only exists in these cases when the custodian fails to use reasonable care.

However, such concepts of duty were not applied to cases of outpatient therapy until the landmark Tarasoff[7,8] cases that extended the concept of a special relationship to outpatient psychotherapy. As is well known, in 1969, Tatiana Tarasoff was killed by a rejected potential lover, Prosenjit Poddar. He had earlier sought outpatient treatment and his preoccupation with Ms. Tarasoff convinced the treating psychologist of his potential dangerousness. After a psychiatric consultation, he notified the police that Mr. Poddar should be taken to a commitment evaluation facility. After interviewing Poddar, the police decided to warn him to stay away from Ms. Tarasoff and let him go. The facility director instructed that no further action be taken. Two months later, after Ms. Tarasoff returned from a foreign trip, Mr. Poddar killed her. In Tarasoff I, the California Supreme Court decided that the special relationship between the therapist and Poddar gave the therapist the duty to warn Ms. Tarasoff. In Tarasoff II, the California Supreme Court expanded upon the duty of the therapist as a "special duty" to Ms. Tarasoff that obligated warning her of the potential danger.

Eagle and Kirkman (1990), state that when a jurisdiction adopts the "special relationship test," Tarasoff related cases generally fall into two areas: (1) Those involving a breach of duty to disclose confidential information to a potential victim or failing to act to prevent harm and

(2) improper discharge of a potentially dangerous patient or youth. As is well known to mental health practitioners, many states have followed the Tarasoff test (especially the Tarasoff II standard of "special relationship") in determination of liability in cases of duty to warn.[9-11] As well, the standard has been followed in federal appeals courts.[12,13]

POST TARASOFF LEGISLATIVE RESPONSES

Following this decision, some states modified their statutes to allow psychotherapists protection, or immunity, from negligence or malpractice claims in cases of duty to warn. To illustrate, in what was termed "the most sweeping Anti-Tarasoff statute in the nation" (Eagle and Kirkman, 1990), Ohio revised many of its mental health laws in the 1988 Mental Health Act. The resultant changes significantly revised limitations upon confidentiality and provided a limited exception to the duty of confidentiality in order to protect the youth from committing acts dangerous to himself or others. The Ohio Revised Code, section 5122.34, states: "No person shall be liable for any harm that results to another person as a result of failing to disclose any confidential information about a mental health youth or failing to otherwise attempt to protect such a person from harm by such youth." This statute provided what was thought to be essentially unqualified immunity to mental health professionals from liability for failure to warn or protect a third party victim and potentially eliminates liability for negligent discharge of a patient.

Recent Judicial Limitations on Tarasoff

The second key issue is that of "good faith actions" on the part of psychotherapists. In Ohio, for example, in the case of Littleton v. Good Samaritan, the Ohio Supreme Court previously limited liability in negligent discharges to cases in which the physician acts in bad faith or fails to exercise good judgment. In Littleton, a psychiatrist and hospital were sued for negligent release after a patient murdered her infant shortly after discharge. She had been diagnosed as suffering from recurring depression and had been discharged under an extensive outpatient program that included outpatient therapy and family involvement. This included a warning to the family that she had the potential to harm her child and that she should not be left alone with the infant. Two weeks later, the family allowed her to watch the child alone and she administered a fatal dose of aspirin to the child. In Littleton, the court held that the psychiatrist did have a special duty to prevent reasonably foreseeable harm as a result of the special duty. However, the court adopted a "professional judgment standard" that stated that a psychiatrist could not be held liable if she evaluated all relevant information and reached, in good faith, a professional judgment that the patient did not pose a risk of harm to self or others. As a result, the court found for the defense in this case. The court held that there is no liability for violence after discharge if there is a thorough evaluation and good faith determination that patient is not a danger.

However, In a potentially far-reaching decision, the Ohio Supreme Court, in the case of *Estates of Morgan v. Fairfield Family Counseling Center* (1997), 77 Ohio St.3d 284,[14] virtually eliminated any legal protections once thought to be allowed outpatient mental health clinicians against liability for harmful actions of their patients. This recent decision has the clear potential to serve as precedent for other states. It expands the common law concept of duty between the patient and "psychotherapist" to that of a "special relationship." It states that there is a resultant duty that if the psychotherapist either knows or should know that his or her outpatient represents a substantial risk of harm to others. If this condition exists, then the therapist is under a specific duty to exercise his or her best professional judgment to prevent such harm from occurring.

Further, this decision will potentially expose thousands of mental health professionals in Ohio and other states to liability only if they choose to not hospitalize the patient. Mental Health professionals in Ohio are now potentially subject to civil damages liability for preventing and even controlling the potential violent potentials of their patients even in the absence of specific threats made against individuals. This potential exists even if the professional made a good faith determination that hospitalization was not indicated. Lastly, this decision sidesteps current Ohio Legislation (Ohio Revised Code 5122.34) that had previously granted immunity to mental health professionals in cases of duty to warn.

Useful Stuff and an Afterword: How to Find a Good Mechanic

This is a handout/outline that I have found helpful in working with aggressive youth and their families/teachers, counselors, etc.

METHODS OF NONVIOLENT CONFLICT RESOLUTION

1. *Focus upon the problem,* not the person. Remember that the issue is between two people, not the persons themselves.
2. *Keep an open mind.* It is far too easy to think that things are the way that we see them. There are many ways to solve a problem.
3. *Take time to hear the other person.* Listen and try to learn the other's perspective. Listen for both the content and the feeling of what the person is saying.
4. *Use humor.* Things are often not as important as we first believe them to be. The use of humor at the right time can often diffuse a potentially volatile situation. Remember though, that humor can also be a weapon and choose your words carefully so as not to worsen conflict.
5. *Plan ahead.* Slow down; think ahead before you enter a potentially violent situation.
6. *Think peacefully.* Thoughts that cause us to become angry and potentially violent are "hot thoughts." "Cool thoughts" are those that focus upon nonviolent resolutions. For every "hot thought," there is a "cool thought."
7. *Slow down.* Don't rush into a problem. If you feel yourself being swept along in an emotional rush, then step back, calm yourself, and wait until the anger passes and remain open to compromise.

8. *Avoid the conflict.* Often what seems important to us at the moment of conflict loses value later when the intensity passes. There are times when it takes more courage to leave than to stay. Don't place yourself in situations in which you are likely to become angry. If you cannot avoid it, then plan for a non-violent strategy. If you are surprised, tell yourself that you always are in control of how you respond.

9. *Reduce the cues.* Research has consistently shown that cues, or triggers to aggression result in an increase in violent behavior, especially when emotions are strong. Do not keep weapons available to children; remove posters and signs that advocate violence.

10. *Control the environment.* Exposure to aggressive role models increases the likelihood of aggressive behavior by those who observe the person. Parents must control the media that surround children. Do not allow children to watch excessive violence on television. Listen carefully to the lyrics of popular music. Do not be afraid to limit access but be sure to explain your reasons.

11. *Humanize.* Violence against other persons happens most often when we do not see the other as equal to ourselves, as deserving of respect. Actively combat attitudes and values that promote racism, sexism, and abuse.

In the home, parents can do many things to help prevent violence:

1. Be a positive role model.
2. Turn off television violence. Teach children to monitor the content of TV programs.
3. Take the time to explain to children acceptable ways to deal with anger. Teach them that violence is but *one* response to anger. Remember that anger can be a helpful emotion. It is not anger that causes us problems. We often have a right to be angry. It is what we do with that anger that causes problems. Children should be taught to neither act out violence in an aggressive way or to hold in their anger.
4. Parents should not only discourage violent behavior but reward nonviolent problem resolution. "Catch them being

good—nonviolent" and praise them. Even the seemingly most self-assured teenager seeks out the attention and approval of parents. Parents can use this fact of psychological development to encourage the development of a nonviolent lifestyle.

5. Set limits, discourage aggressive behavior. Be consistent in discipline and remember that the purpose of discipline is not to punish bad behavior but to teach positive skills. Avoid the use of physical punishment that only gives license to the child to respond aggressively to interpersonal situations.

6. Teach children to talk, to solve problems, and resolve conflicts nonviolently. Don't just tell children how they should act. Instead, give them skills, strategies, and examples.

7. Expose children to persons of other cultures and values. Let them get to know others as different but not their lessor. Encourage diversity and actively discourage racism and sexism. Remember that children are as sponges, taking in your values far more than what is seen at the moment.

8. Encourage teachers and community leaders to develop nonviolent solutions to problems. Become active in school and community events.

9. Listen to your children. Allow them to develop a sense of self-respect and individuality. Encourage them to be independent but first teach them skills and how to choose.

10. Deemphasize material values.

We are not powerless. There are many things that we as parents, counselors and teachers can do to prevent violence in our society and in the society of the future.

HELPING THE HELPER

My grandfather was a railroad mechanic. From him, I learned that a good mechanic can be identified by how the mechanic takes care of his or her tools. In mental health, we have few other tools than ourselves. Interventions with violent youth are difficult and have the potential for considerable interpersonal cost to the clinician. We need to remember that we, too, have limits, feelings, values, and priorities.

An effective clinician is sensitive to those needs and avoids becoming so enmeshed that one's needs are met through clinical services, or to the other extreme, so distanced that clinical services are neglected. Counselors should set an active plan to take care of themselves. A balancing hobby or some sort of relaxing passion is nearly vital to success in this profession. Take time to refresh, renew. There is much to enjoy about your work and your youth, if you allow yourself.

References

American Psychological Association. (1993). *Violence and youth: Psychology's response*. Washington DC: The American Psychological Association.

American Psychiatric Association. (1994). *Diagnostic and statistical manual of mental disorders* (Fourth edition). Washington, DC: The American Psychiatric Association.

Axelrods, S. and Wetzler, S. (1989). Factors associated with better compliance with psychiatric aftercare. *Hospital and Community Psychiatry, 40*(4), 397-401.

Axelrods, S. and Wetzler, S. (1989). Factors associated with better compliance with psychiatric aftercare. *Hospital and Community Psychiatry, 40*(4), 397-401.

Ball, E., Young, D., Dotson, L., and Brothers, L. (1994), Factors associated with dangerous behavior in forensic inpatients: Results from a pilot study. *Bulletin of the American Academy of Psychiatry and the Law, 22*(4), 605-620.

Bandura, A., Shunk, D.H. (1981). Cultivating competence, self-efficacy, and intrinsic interest through proximal self-motivation. *Journal of Personality and Social Psychology, 41*(?), 586-598.

Bender L. (1959) "Children and adolescents who kill." *American Journal of Psychiatry,* 116-410-413.

Benedek, E.P. (1992). "Adolescent homicide/victims and victimizers." In D.H. Schetky and E.P. Benedek (Eds.), *Clinical Handbook of Child Psychiatry and Law.* Baltimore, MD: Williams and Wilkins.

Ben-Porath, Y. and Davis, D.L. (1996). *An MMPI-A casebook.* Minneapolis: University of Minnesota Press.

Boreland, A., McRae, J., and Lycan, C. (1989). Outcomes of five years of continuous, intensive case management. *Hospital and Community Psychiatry, 40*(4), 369-376.

Borum, R. (????). Improving the clinical practice of violence risk assessment. *American Psychologist, 51*(?), 945-956.

Bridges, K.M.B. (1933). "A study of social development in early infancy." *Child Development, 4*(?), 36-39.

Brodsky, S.L. (1973). *Psychologists in the criminal justice system.* Urbana: University of Illinois Press.

Brodsky, S.L. (1988). Fear of litigation in mental health professionals. *Criminal Justice and Behavior, 15*(4), 492-500.

Brodsky, S.L. (1991). *Testifying in court.* Washington, DC: American Psychological Association.

Brodsky, S.L. and Fischer, C.T. (Eds.). (1978). *Client participation in the human services: The Prometheus principle.* New Brunswick, NJ: Transaction Books.

Brodsky, S.L., Clements, C., Davis, D.L., Poythress, N.G. (1989). Psychological and psycholegal consequences of lawsuits against institutions. *Symposium Presented at the 97th Annual Convention of the American Psychological Association.*

Brown, A. and Finklehor, D. (1986). Impact of child sexual abuse: A review of the research. *Psychological Bulletin, 99*(?), 66-77.

Busch, K.G., Zagar, R., Hughes, J.R., and Arbit, J. (1990). "Adolescents who kill." *Journal of Clinical Psychology, 46*(4), 472-485.

Calicchia, J., Moncata, S., Santostefano, S. (1993). Cognitive control differences in violent juvenile inpatients. *Journal of Clinical Psychology, 49*(5), 731-740.

Capaldi, D.M. and Patterson, G.R. (1991). "Relation of parental transitions to boys' adjustment problems: I. A linear hypothesis: II. Mothers at risk for transitions and unskilled parenting." *Developmental Psychology, 27*(3), 489-504.

Chen, A. (1991). Noncompliance in community psychiatry: A review of clinical interventions. *Hospital and Community Psychiatry, 42*(3), 282-286.

Circincione, C., Steadman, H., Robbins, P., and Monahan, J. (1992). Schizophrenia as a risk factor for criminal violence. *International Journal of Law and Psychiatry, 15*(4), 347-358.

Convit, I. and Otis, V. (1990). Characteristics of repeatedly assaultive psychiatric inpatients. *Hospital and Community Psychiatry, 41*(10), 1112-1116.

Cooper, D.K. (1997). "Juvenile's understanding of trial-related information: Are they competent defendants?" *Behavioral Sciences and the Law, 15*(2), 167-180.

Cornel, D., Benedek, E., and Benedek, D. (1987). "Characteristics of adolescents charged with homicide: Review of 72 cases." *Behavioral Sciences and the Law, 5*(1), 11-23.

Cornel, D., Benedek, E., and Benedek, D. (1987). "Juvenile Homicide: Prior Adjustment and a Proposed Typology. *American Journal of Orthopsychiatry, 57*(3), 383-393.

Cornel, D.G., Miller, C., Benedek, E.P., (1988). "MMPI Profiles of Adolescents charged with Homicide. *Behavioral Sciences and the Law, 6*(3), 401-407.

Cornell D.G. (1990). "Prior adjustment of violent juvenile offenders." *Law and Human Behavior, 14*(6), 569-577.

Corrigan, P., Liberman, R.P., and Engel, J.D. (1990). From noncompliance to collaboration in the treatment of schizophrenia. *Hospital and Community Psychiatry, 41*(11), 1203-1211.

Davis, D.L. (1985). "Treatment planning for the patient who is incompetent to stand trial." *Hospital and Community Psychiatry. 34*(3), ??.

Davis, D.L. (1986). "Assessment of competency to stand trial." *Journal of Forensic Psychology, 3*(3), ??.

Davis, D.L. (1992). "Interventions with the aggressive youth." *Innovations in Residential Treatment—1992.* Washington, DC: American Association of Residential Centers for Children.

Davis, D.L., Bean, G.L., Schumacher, J.E., Stringer, T.L. (1991). "Prevalence of emotional disorders in a juvenile justice institutional population." *American Journal of Forensic Psychology, 9*(1), 5-17.

Davis, D.L. and Boster, L.H. (1987). The violent psychiatric inpatient. *American Journal of Forensic Psychology, 4*(1), 3-17.

Davis, D.L. and Boster, L.H. (1988). Multifaceted interventions with the violent psychiatric inpatient. *Hospital and Community Psychiatry, 39*(8), 867-869.

Davis, D.L. and Boster, L.H. (1992). "Cognitive-behavioral-expressive interventions with aggressive and resistant youth." *Child Welfare, LXXI*(6), 557-574.

Davis, D.L. and Boster, L.H. (1993). "Cognitive-behavioral-expressive interventions with aggressive and resistant youth." *Residential Treatment for Children and Youth, 10*(4), 55-68.

Davis, D.L. and Brodsky, S.L. (1992). "Psychotherapy with the unwilling youth." *Residential Treatment for Children and Youth, 9*(3), ??.

Davis, S.D. (1991). "Violence by psychiatric inpatients: A review." *Hospital and Community Psychiatry, 42*(6), 585-590.

Donovan, S.J., Susser, E.S., Nunes E.V., Stewart, J.W. (1997). "Divalproex treatment of disruptive adolescents: A report of 10 cases. *Journal of Clinical Psychiatry, 59*(1), 12-15.

Duncan, J.W. and Duncan, G.M. (1971). "Murder in the family: A study of some homicidal adolescents." *American Journal of Psychiatry, 127*(11), 1498-1502.

Eagle, S.J. and Kirkman, M. (1990). *Ohio mental health law.* Cleveland, OH: Banks-Baldwin Law Publishing Company.

Erikson, E.H. (1959). *Identity and the life cycle: Selected papers.* New York, NY: International Universities Press.

Ewing, C.P. (1990). *When children kill: The dynamics of juvenile homicide.* Lexington, MA: Lexington Books/D.C. Heath and Company.

Faretra, G. and Grad, G.J. (1989). "Special considerations in the inhospital treatment of dangerously violent juveniles." In R. Rosner and H.I. Schwartz (Eds.), *Juvenile psychiatry and the law, Volume 4, Critical issues in American psychiatry and the law* (pp. 333-343). New York: Plenum Press.

Freud, S. (1939). *The standard edition of the complete psychological works of Sigmund Freud, (Volume 21).* London: Hogarth.

Frost L. (1997). *State juvenile code provisions for restoration to competency.* Invited Presentation. National Association of Forensic Center Directors, Annapolis, MD.

Gesell, A. (1954). "The ontogenesis of human behavior." In L. Carmichael (Ed.), *Manual of Child Psychology.* New York: Wiley.

Goodman, G.S. and Hahn, A. (1987). "Evaluating eyewitness testimony." In I.B. Weiner and A.K. Hess (Eds.), *Handbook of Forensic Psychology.* New York: Wiley.

Grisso, T. (1997). "The competence of adolescents as trial defendants." *Public Policy and Law, 3*(1), 3-32.

Grisso, T. (1996). "Society's retributive response to juvenile violence: A developmental perspective." *Law and Human Behavior, 20*(3), 229-247.

Hare, R.D. and Schalling, D (Eds.). (1978). *Psychopathic behavior: Approaches to research.* New York: Wiley.

Hare, R.D. (1991). *The Hare Psychopathy checklist-revised.* Toronto: Multi-Health Systems.

Harris, G.T., Rice, M,E., and Quinsel, V.L. (1993). Violent recidivism of mentally disordered offenders: The development of a statistical prediction instrument. *Criminal Justice and Behavior, 20*(?), 315-335.

Heilbrun, K. (1992). The role of psychological testing in forensic assessment. *Law and Human Behavior, 16*(?), 257-272.

Heilbrun, K. (1993). Risk assessment workshop. Columbus, Ohio: *The Association of Ohio Forensic Center Directors Annual Conference.*

Heilbrun, K., Hawk, G., Tate, DC. (1996), "Juvenile competence to stand trial. Research issues in practice." *Law and Human Behavior, 20*(5), 573-578.

Jemelka, R.P., Rahman, S., and Tupin, E.W. (1993). *"Prison mental health: An overview."* In H.J. Steadman and J.J. Cocozza (Ed.), *Mental Illness in America's Prisons,* Seattle, WA: The National Coalition for the Mentally Ill in the Criminal Justice System.

Kohlberg, L. (1976). *"Moral stages and moralization: The cognitive-developmental approach."* In T. Lickona (Ed.), *Moral Development and Behavior,* New York: Holt, Rinehart and Winston.

Lewis, D.O. (1983). *Vulnerabilities to delinquency,* New York: SP Medical and Scientific Books.

Lewis, D.O., Lovely, R., Yeager, C., and Della Famina, D. (1991). "Toward a theory of the genesis of violence: A follow-up study of delinquents." In S. Chess and M.E. Hertzig (Eds.), *Annual progress in child psychiatry and child development* (pp. 547-560). New York: Brunner/Mazel, Inc. 547-560.

Lewis, D.O., Pincus, J.H., Bard, B., and Richardson, E. (1988). "Neuropsychiatric, psychoeducational, and family characteristics of 14 juveniles condemned to death in the United States." *American Journal of Psychiatry, 145*(5), 584-589.

Lich, J.D., Kavoussi, R.J., and Coccaro, E.F. (1996). *"Aggressive."* In C.G. Costello (Ed.), *Personality characteristics of the personality disordered.* New York: Wiley and Sons.

Link B.G., Andrews, H., and Cullen, F.T. (1992). The violent and illegal behavior of mental patients reconsidered. *American Sociological Review, 57*(??), 275-292.

Link, B.G. and Stueve, A. (1995). Evidence bearing on mental illness as a possible cause of violent behavior. *Epidemiological Reviews, 17*(??), 1-10.

Lochman, J.E., White, kJ., and Wayland, KK. (1990). *"Cognitive-behavioral assessment and treatment with aggressive children."* In P.C. Kendall (Ed.), *Child and Youth therapy: Cognitive-behavioral procedures.* New York: Guilford Press.

Loftus, E.F. (1979). *Eyewitness testimony.* Cambridge MA: Harvard University Press.

McKee, G.R. (1998). "Competency to stand trial in preadjudicatory juveniles and adults." *Bulletin of the American Academy of Psychiatry and the Law, 26*(1), 89-99.

McCord, J. (1980). "Patterns of deviance." In S.B. Sells, R. Crandall, M. Roff, J.S. Strauss, and W. Pollin (Eds.), *Human functioning in longitudinal perspective.* Baltimore: Williams and Wilkins.

McGarry A.L., et al. (1973). Competency to stand trial and mental illness. Washington DC: U.S. Government Printing Office.

Megargee, E.I. (1988). "Derivation, validation, and application of an MMPI-based system for classifying criminal youth." *Medicine and Law, 3*(??), 109-118.

Melton, G.B., Petrila, J., Poythress, N.G., and Slobogin, C. (1997). *Psychological evaluations for the courts: A handbook for mental health professionals and lawyers* (Second edition). New York: The Guilford Press.

Monahan, J. and Steadman, H. (1996). Violent storms and violent people: How meteorology can inform risk communication in mental health law. *American Psychologist, 51*(??), 931-938.

Monahan, J. (1981). *The Clinical Prediction of Violent Behavior.* Beverly Hills, CA: Sage Publications.

Monahan, J. (1992). Mental disorder and violent behavior: Perceptions and evidence. *American Psychologist, 48*(??), 242-250.

Monahan, J. and Steadman, H. (Eds.). (1994). *Violence and mental disorder: Developments in risk assessment.* Chicago, IL: University of Chicago Press.

Mulvey, E.P. (1994). "Assessing the evidence of a link between mental illness and violence." *Hospital and Community Psychiatry, 45*(??), 663-668.

Mulvey, E.P. and Wollard, J.L. (1997). "Themes for consideration in future research on prevention and intervention with antisocial behaviors." In D.M. Stoff and J. Breiling (Eds.), *Handbook of antisocial behavior.* New York: Wiley.

Myers, W.C., Burgess, A.W., and Nelson, J.A. (1998). "Criminal and behavioral aspects of juvenile sexual homicide. *Journal of Forensic Sciences, 43*(2) 340-347.

Myers, W.C., Scott, K., Burgess, A.W., and Burgess, A.G. (1995). Psychopathology, biopsychosocial factors, crime characteristics, and classification of 25 homicidal youth. *Journal of the American Academy of Child and Adolescent Psychiatry, 34*(11), 1483-1490.

National Juvenile Custody Trends 1978-1989. (1992). United States Department of Justice.

Novaco, R. (1975). *Anger Control: The Development and Evaluation of an Experimental Treatment.* Lexington, MA: DC Heath, Lexington Books.

Olfson, M. (1990). Assertive community treatment: An evaluation of the evidence. *Hospital and Community Psychiatry, 41*(6), 634-641.

Ornstein, R.E. (1986). *The Psychology of Consciousness.* New York: Pelican Books.

Otto, R. (1992). The prediction of dangerous behavior: A review and analysis of "second generation" research. *Forensic Reports, 5*(??), 103-133.

Otto, R.K., Greenstein, J.J., and Friedman R.M. (1992). *"Prevalence of mental disorders in the juvenile justice system."* In J.J. Cocozza (Ed.), *Responding to the mental health needs of youth in the juvenile justice system.* Seattle, WA: The National Coalition for the Mentally Ill in the Criminal Justice System.

Patterson, G.R., Capaldi, D., and Bank, L. (1991). "An early starter model for predicting delinquency." In D.J. Pepler and K.H. Ruben (Eds.), *The development and treatment of childhood aggression* (pp. 139-168). Hillsdale, NJ: Lawrence Erlbaum Associates. .

Patterson, G.R., DeBaryshe, B.D., and Ransey, E. (1989). "A developmental perspective on antisocial behavior." *The American Psychologist, 44*(2), 329-335.

Pepler, D.J. and Slaby, R.G. (1994). "Theoretical and developmental perspectives on youth and violence." In L.D. Eron, J.H. Gentry, and P. Schlegel (Eds.), *Reason to hope: A psychosocial perspective on violence and youth* (pp. 27-58). Washington, DC: American Psychological Association.

Piaget, J. (1963). *The Origins of Intelligence in Children.* New York: Norton.

Pinta, E. and Davis, D.L. (1987). Interventions with violent patients. *Grand Rounds Presentation,* Department of Psychiatry, College of Medicine, The Ohio State University.

Poythress, N.G. (1987). Avoiding negligent release: A risk-management strategy. *Hospital and Community Psychiatry, 38*(10), 1051-1052.

Quinn, M.M., Mathur, S.R., and Rutherford, R.B. (1991). "Early identification of antisocial boys: A multi-method approach." *Special issue: Severe behavior disorders of children and youth* (Volume 18).

Reid, J.B. and Patterson, G.R. (1989). "The development of antisocial behavior patterns in childhood and adolescence." *European Journal of Psychology.*

Resnick, P. (1993). *Diagnosis of malingering.* Invited presentation. Ohio Association of Forensic Directors Association.

Resnick P. (1995). *Competency and sanity.* Invited presentation. Ohio Department of Mental Health.

Resnick, P. (1995). *Duty to protect potential victims.* Invited presentation. Ohio Department of Mental Health.

Resnick, P.J. (1997). Malingering of posttraumatic disorders. In R. Rogers (Ed.), *Clinical assessment of malingering and deception* (Second edition). New York: Guilford Press.

Rice, M. and Harris G.T. (1992). "A comparison of criminal recidivism among schizophrenic and nonschizophrenic offenders." *International Journal of Law and Psychiatry, 15*(??), 397-408.

Roesch, R. and Golding, S.L. (1980). Competency to stand trial. Chicago, IL: University of Chicago Press.

Serin, R. and Amos, N. (1995). The role of psychopathy in the assessment of dangerousness. *International Journal of Law and Psychiatry, 18*(2), 231-238.

Shamsie, J., Hamilton, H., and Sykes, C. (1996), "The characteristics and intervention histories of incarcerated and conduct-disordered youth." *Canadian Journal of Psychiatry, 41*(4), 211-216.

Shaw, R.E., Hargreaves, W., Surber, R., and Luft, L. (1990). Continuity of intensity of case management activity in three community mental health centers. *Hospital and Community Psychiatry, 41*(3), 323-325.

Snow, K. (1994). "Aggression: Just part of the job? The psychological impact of aggression on child and youth workers." *Journal of Child and Youth Care, 9*(4), 11-29.

Steadman, H. (1979). *Beating a rap? Defendants found incompetent to stand trial.* Chicago: University of Chicago Press.

Steadman, H., Mulvey, E., Monahan, J., Robbins, P., Appelbaum, P., Grisso, T., Roth, L., and Silver, E. (1998). "Violence by people discharged from acute psychiatric inpatient facilities and by others in the same neighborhoods." *Archives of General Psychiatry, 55*(??), 1-9.

Swanson, J.W. (1994). "Mental disorder substance abuse and community violence: An epidemiological approach." In J. Monahan and H. Steadman (Eds.), *Violence and mental disorder: Developments in risk assessment.* Chicago: University of Chicago Press.

Tardiff, K., Marzuk, P.M., Leon, A.C., Portera, L., and Weiner, C. (1997). "Violence by patients admitted to a private psychiatric hospital." *American Journal of Psychiatry, 154*(1), 88-93.

Tate, D.C., Reppucci, N.D., and Mulvey, E.P. (1996). "Violent juvenile delinquents: Treatment effectiveness and implications for future action. *American Psychologist, 50*(9), 777-781.

Toch, H. (1982). The disturbed, disruptive youth: Where does the bus stop? *The Journal of Psychiatry and Law, ?*(?), 327-349.

Toch, H. and Adams, K. (1987). The prison as dumping ground: Mainlining disturbed youth. *The Journal of Psychiatry and Law, ?*(?),539-553.

Warboys, L. and Wilber, S. (1997). "Mental health issues in juvenile justice." In B. Sales and D.W. Shuman (Eds.), *Law, mental health, and mental disorder.* Pacific Groves, CA: Brooks/Cole Publishing Company.

Weinberger, D.A. and Gomes, M.E. (1998). Changes in daily mood and self-restraint among undercontrolled preadolescents: A time-series analysis of "acting out." *Journal of the American Academy of Child and Adolescent Psychiatry, 34*(11), 1473-1482.

Williams, C.L., Butcher, J.N., Ben-Porath, Y.L., and Graham, J.R. (1992). MMIP-A content scales: Assessing psychopathology in adolescents. Minneapolis, MN: University of Minnesota Press.

Woody, R.H. (1988). *Public policy, malpractice law, and the mental health professional: Some legal and clinical guidelines.* In C.P. Ewing (Ed.), *Psychology, psychiatry, and the law: A clinical and forensic handbook.* Sarasota: Professional Resources Press.

Legal Citations

1. Kent v. U.S. 383, U.S. 541 (1966)

2. In re Gault, 387 U.S. 1 (1967)

3. Dusky v. United States, 362 U.S. 402 (1960)

4. Rex v. Braiser (11 Leach 199, 168 Eng Rep. 202, 1779)

5. Wheeler v. United States (159 US 523, 1985)

6. Littleton v. Good Samaritan Hospital, 39, OS(3d) 86, 529, NE(2d) 449 (1988)

7. Tarasoff v. Regents of University of California, 13, Cal(3d) 177, 188 Cal Rptr 553, 529 P(2d) 553 (1974)

8. Tarasoff v. Regents of University of California, 13, Cal(3d) 177, 188 Cal Rptr 553, 529 P(2d) 553 (1974)

9. Macintosh v. Milano, 168 NJ Super 466, 403 A(2d) 500 (1979)

10. Davis v. Lhim, 124 Mich App 291, 335 NW (2d) 481 (1983)

11. Mavroudis v. Superior Court, 102 Cal App(3d) 594, 162 Cal Rptr 724 (1980)

12. Jablonski v. United States, 712 F(2d) 391 (9th Cir Cal 1983)

13. Sellers v. United States, 870 F(2d) 1098 (6th Cir Mich 1989)

14. Estates of Morgan v. Fairfield Family Counseling Center (1997), 77 Ohio St.3d 284